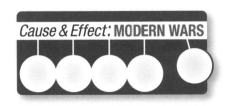

Cause & Effect: MODERN WARS

Cause & Effect: World War II

Hal Marcovitz

ReferencePoint Press®

San Diego, CA

About the Author

Hal Marcovitz is a former newspaper reporter and columnist. He has written more than 180 books for young readers. He makes his home in Chalfont, Pennsylvania.

For more information, contact:
ReferencePoint Press, Inc.
PO Box 27779
San Diego, CA 92198
www.ReferencePointPress.com

LIBRARY OF CONGRESS CATALOGING-IN-PUBLICATION DATA

Name: Marcovitz, Hal, author.
Title: Cause & Effect. World War II/by Hal Marcovitz.
Description: San Diego, CA: ReferencePoint Press, Inc., 2018. | Series:
   Cause & Effect: Modern Wars series | Includes bibliographical references
   and index.
Identifiers: LCCN 2017007633 (print) | LCCN 2017008049 (ebook) | ISBN
   9781682821749 (hardback) | ISBN 9781682821756 (eBook)
Subjects: LCSH: World War, 1939–1945—Juvenile literature. | World War,
   1939–1945—Causes—Juvenile literature. | World War, 1939–1945—United
   States—Juvenile literature.
Classification: LCC D743.7 .M355 2018 (print) | LCC D743.7 (ebook) | DDC
   940.53/1--dc23
LC record available at https://lccn.loc.gov/2017007633

CONTENTS

"History is a complex study of the many causes that have influenced happenings of the past and the complicated effects of those varied causes."

—William & Mary School of Education,
Center for Gifted Education

U nderstanding the causes and effects of historical events, including those that occur within the context of war, is rarely simple. The Cold War's Cuban Missile Crisis, for instance, resulted from a complicated—and at times convoluted—series of events set in motion by US, Soviet, and Cuban actions. And that crisis, in turn, shaped interactions between the United States and the former Soviet Union for years to come. Had any of these events not taken place or had they occurred under different circumstances, the effects might have been something else altogether.

The value of analyzing cause and effect in the context of modern wars, therefore, is not necessarily to identify a single cause for a singular event. The real value lies in gaining a greater understanding of history as a whole and being able to recognize the many factors that give shape and direction to historic events. As outlined by the National Center for History in the Schools at the University of California–Los Angeles, these factors include "the importance of the individual in history . . . the influence of ideas, human interests, and beliefs; and . . . the role of chance, the accidental and the irrational."

ReferencePoint's Cause & Effect: Modern Wars series examines wars of the modern age by focusing on specific causes and consequences. For instance, in *Cause & Effect (Modern Wars): The Cold War*, a chapter explores whether the US military buildup in the 1980s helped end the Cold War. And in *Cause & Effect (Modern Wars): The Vietnam War*, one chapter delves into this question: "How Did Fear of Communism Lead to US Intervention in Vietnam?" Every book in the series includes thoughtful discussion of questions like these—supported by facts, examples, and a mix of fully documented primary and secondary source quotes. Each title also includes an overview of the event so that readers have a broad context for understanding the more detailed discussions of specific causes and their effects.

The value of such study is not limited to the classroom; it can also be applied to many areas of contemporary life. The ability to analyze and interpret history's causes and consequences is a form of critical thinking. Critical thinking is crucial in many professions, ranging from law enforcement to science. Critical thinking is also essential for developing an educated citizenry that fully understands the rights and obligations of living in a free society. The ability to sift through and analyze complex processes and events and identify their possible outcomes enables people in that society to make important decisions.

The Cause & Effect: Modern Wars series has two primary goals. One is to help students think more critically about history and develop a true understanding of its complexities. The other is to help build a foundation for those students to become fully participating members of the society in which they live.

IMPORTANT EVENTS OF WORLD WAR II

1921
Hitler is named leader of the Nazi Party.

1918
On November 11 World War I ends; German troops return home convinced they were betrayed by cowardly and duplicitous leaders.

1938
At the Munich Conference, British prime minister Neville Chamberlain agrees to Hitler's demands for Czechoslovakia to turn over the Sudetenland to Germany.

1937
Japanese troops sweep into China, gaining control over most of the country.

| 1919 | 1923 | 1927 | 1931 | 1935 | 1939 |

1919
The Treaty of Versailles is signed June 24 at a palace outside Paris, compelling Germany to pay $32 billion in war reparations; Adolf Hitler joins the Nazi Party.

1924
Hitler and the Nazis attempt to overthrow the Bavarian state government; the coup fails.

1933
After Nazi candidates gain control of the Reichstag, Hitler is named chancellor of Germany.

1923
In response to Germany's plan to repay its war debt in worthless currency, French troops invade the Ruhr in Germany, seizing coal and shipping it back to France.

1939
German troops invade Poland, touching off World War II.

1922
Fascist dictator Benito Mussolini seizes power in Italy.

6

1940

The Germans invade France; on May 26 the evacuation at Dunkirk commences, saving 338,000 British, French, and Belgian troops from death or capture by the Germans. On September 22 Japan invades French Indochina.

1944

The June 6 invasion of Normandy lands 150,000 Allied troops in France.

1943

Meeting in Tehran, Iran, US president Franklin D. Roosevelt, British prime minister Winston Churchill, and Soviet leader Joseph Stalin agree to open a second front against the Germans in France.

1948

The Marshall Plan is launched, providing $13 billion in aid to war-torn Europe; to protest the Marshall Plan, the Soviets create a blockade around the city of Berlin.

1949

The Soviets call off the blockade after US and British military planes fly 2.3 million tons (2.1 million metric tons) of food into the city.

1940   1942   1944   1946   1948   1950

1951

Aid under the Marshall Plan ends, but competition among Soviets and the Western democracies for European domination persists for another four decades until the collapse of the Soviet Union in 1991.

1945

On May 7 Germany surrenders after Soviet and Allied troops close in on Berlin; on August 14 Japan surrenders after the cities of Hiroshima and Nagasaki are destroyed by atomic bombs.

1941

On June 22 Hitler orders an invasion of the Soviet Union; America enters the war following the December 7 attack on Pearl Harbor by Japanese planes.

Appeasement at Munich

When British prime minister Neville Chamberlain arrived in the German city of Munich on September 29, 1938, his aim was to avoid war at any cost. For months German dictator Adolf Hitler had been threatening to invade neighboring Czechoslovakia. Publicly, Hitler claimed his aim was to free more than 3 million ethnic Germans living in the Sudetenland, a region of Czechoslovakia along Germany's southeastern border. But Hitler harbored a far more sinister plan: He intended to crush Czechoslovakia as he pushed German borders outward with the goal of making Germany the most powerful and feared nation in Europe.

> "However much we may sympathize with a small nation confronted by a big and powerful neighbor, we cannot in all circumstances undertake to involve the whole British Empire in a war simply on her account."[1]
>
> —British prime minister Neville Chamberlain

Hitler had already accomplished the first step in his plan months earlier when he sent troops into neighboring Austria to annex the country, making it part of Germany. Hitler's policy was known as *Anschluss*—the unification of all German-speaking peoples. On March 12, when German troops occupied the Austrian capital of Vienna, leaders of Europe's two major democracies—Great Britain and France—voiced protests but took no further action to maintain Austria's sovereignty. But now, as Hitler moved against Czechoslovakia, British and French leaders realized they had to halt Hitler's aggression or the Continent would be plunged into war.

Chamberlain knew there were only two ways to deal with the crisis: negotiate a settlement or commit British and French troops to the defense of Czechoslovakia. Certainly, a war would be costly. Two decades earlier, nearly 1 million British troops and 1.3 million French troops died in the four-year conflict against Germany known today as World War I. Chamberlain, a dedicated pacifist, believed he could halt German aggression through diplomatic channels. He offered to meet with Hitler, and a summit was scheduled for September 29 in Munich.

Conference in Munich

The Munich Conference was attended by Chamberlain and Hitler, as well as Édouard Daladier, the premier of France, and Benito Mussolini, the dictator of Italy and a Hitler ally. Czechoslovakian leaders demanded their country be given a seat at the conference table, but they were refused. Indeed, Chamberlain had no interest in using military force to defend Czechoslovakia's sovereignty—and as the conference neared, he left little doubt about how he intended to settle the Sudetenland crisis. "However much we may sympathize with a small nation confronted by a big and powerful neighbor, we cannot in all circumstances undertake to involve the whole British Empire in a war simply on her account," Chamberlain declared on September 27, two days before the start of the conference. "If we must fight it must be on larger issues than that."[1]

Early in the morning of September 30, Hitler, Chamberlain, Daladier, and Mussolini emerged from the Munich negotiations to announce they had resolved the Sudetenland crisis. The region would be turned over to Germany. Learning of the outcome of the conference, the outraged Czechoslovakian president, Edvard Beneš, said, "We have been basely betrayed."[2]

Adolf Hitler arrives in the Sudetenland to cheering crowds in 1938. Some historians now believe that if England and France had opposed Hitler at this point, World War II may have been avoided.

The policy embraced by Chamberlain—and endorsed by Daladier—is known as appeasement. Essentially, the leaders of Europe's two major democracies concluded that the autocratic Hitler would cease his aggressiveness if they agreed fully to his demands. And while Chamberlain was cheered days later upon his return to London for keeping his country out of war, some British political leaders were horrified by the terms of the Munich Agreement—predicting that it would fail to halt Hitler's intentions to conquer Europe. Speaking in the British Parliament on October 5, 1938, opposition leader Winston Churchill said:

> "We are in the presence of a disaster of the first magnitude which has befallen Great Britain and France."[3]
>
> —Winston Churchill

> We are in the presence of a disaster of the first magnitude which has befallen Great Britain and France. Do not let us blind ourselves to that. . . . Many people, no doubt, honestly believe that they are only giving away the interests of Czechoslovakia, whereas I fear we shall find that we have deeply compromised, and perhaps fatally endangered, the safety and even the independence of Great Britain and France.[3]

As Churchill predicted, the Munich Agreement did not halt Hitler's plans. In March 1939 the dictator sent his troops into the remainder of Czechoslovakia, occupying the entire country and taking control of its coal mines; iron, steel and cement industries; chemical and textile factories; and thousands of acres of timberland—all resources necessary to equip an army and wage war throughout Europe. Again, Chamberlain and his French allies did nothing to halt Hitler's aggression. Only after Germany invaded Poland in September 1939 did Britain and France finally declare war on Germany.

A Fatal Mistake

Looking back, historians believe that in September 1938, Hitler lacked the resources to fight off the British and French armies if they had elected to send their troops to oppose the occupation of the Sudetenland. William L. Shirer, a journalist stationed in Germany during the era, later wrote, "It was this writer's impression . . . that had Chamberlain frankly told Hitler that Britain would do what it ultimately did in the face of Nazi aggression, [Hitler] would never have embarked on the adventures that brought on the Second World War. . . . This was the well-meaning Prime Minister's fatal mistake."[4]

Indeed, committing troops to an invasion of Czechoslovakia would have forced Hitler to leave his country's western front virtually unprotected, meaning British and French troops could have easily swept into Germany—a fact that Chamberlain's generals made clear to the prime minister. Instead, Chamberlain wished to avoid war at any cost—and chose instead a policy of appeasement. It was a policy that helped lead the world into history's most devastating war.

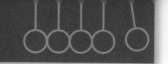

CHAPTER ONE

A Brief History of World War II

The battles of World War II were not fought on every continent. Nor did every country on earth send troops into combat; many countries remained neutral. But by virtually every other measure, World War II was truly a global conflict.

As many as 80 million people—about 3 percent of the world population—died as a result of World War II. That number includes not only troops lost on battlefields but civilians, who were for the first time widely targeted by enemy bombers, submarines, and other devastating weapons. In Europe millions of innocent people died in concentration camps—including 6 million European Jews, targets of Nazi Germany's racist ideology. Whole cities were reduced to rubble by enemy bombers. Meanwhile, large swaths of the Asian continent were overrun by Japanese troops, who murdered and enslaved millions of people while milking their nations of raw materials and natural resources. Enemy ships and submarines faced one another on the world's oceans—from the North Atlantic to the South Pacific. Moreover, the war endured for six years and ended only after the US military unleashed the most devastating weapon known to civilization: the atomic bomb. As the late historian Stephen E. Ambrose wrote, "It was history's greatest catastrophe. More than seventy years after it ended—years marked by constant conflict in at least some parts of the world and by enormous improvements in weaponry and firepower—World War II remains by far the most costly war of all time."[5]

Life Changed

American cities were never targeted by enemy troops, but nevertheless, life in America changed dramatically following the US entry into the war in late 1941. Sixteen million American men ages eighteen to forty-five served in the armed forces. More than 2 million women took the places of their husbands, boyfriends, and brothers in factories, shipyards, and similar industrialized work sites, many of which were retooled to produce weapons. Americans rationed food during the conflict to ensure there would be sufficient supplies to ship overseas to the troops. Cities established air raid shelters and often conducted drills, requiring people to hide in basements, subways, and similar subterranean places. Blackouts—nights when everyone turned off the lights at home—were not uncommon. Blackouts were ordered out of fear that enemy bombers could target bright city lights at night. Along the coasts, Civilian Defense volunteers kept watch for enemy submarines.

Even Major League Baseball shut down during the war, although President Franklin D. Roosevelt asked team owners to keep playing, believing the game was good for national morale. Nevertheless, Major League Baseball was not played during the war, partially out of the dedication by team owners to support the war effort, but also because some five hundred players were serving in the military.

> "More than seventy years after it ended—years marked by constant conflict in at least some parts of the world and by enormous improvements in weaponry and firepower—World War II remains by far the most costly war of all time."[5]
>
> —Stephen E. Ambrose, historian

Nazi-Soviet Pact

By the time America entered the war, the conflict had already been under way for more than two years. Although Great Britain and France failed to respond following the German invasions of Austria and Czechoslovakia, Hitler's aggression against Poland finally convinced the two democracies that the German leader aimed to conquer all of Europe. And so, following the September 3, 1939, invasion of Poland, the two Allies declared war on Germany.

It would be months, however, before French or British troops faced the Germans on the battlefield. Neither nation was prepared for combat. The Allies hoped the Poles could tie up the Germans, giving them

time to field their own armies. But the Polish army was ill equipped to repel the Germans. The German air force, known as the Luftwaffe—literally, German for "air weapon"—initiated a relentless bombing campaign of Polish cities. Moreover, Hitler signed a nonaggression pact with Joseph Stalin, the authoritarian leader of the Soviet Union. The pact forged a bond between Germany and the Soviet Union, specifying that they would be allies in the campaign against Poland. The pact also included an agreement to divide Poland between Germany and the Soviets. On September 17 Soviet troops poured across Poland's eastern border. On September 27 the Polish capital of Warsaw fell to the Nazis.

> "Act brutally, 80 million [Germans] must obtain what is their right."[6]
>
> —Adolf Hitler

Hitler had no intention of sharing Poland with the Soviets, however. Soon after agreeing to the pact with Stalin, Hitler summoned his generals and told them, "Act brutally, 80 million [Germans] must obtain what is their right. . . . Poland will be depopulated and settled with Germans."[6]

Battle of Britain

After capturing Poland, the German army moved next against Denmark, Norway, the Netherlands, Belgium, and Luxembourg. Finally, on May 12, 1940, the Germans invaded France. By now, a force of some two hundred thousand British troops had landed in France to bolster the French defenses, but Germany's superior tank corps—known as the panzers—easily overran the defenders and pushed British, French, and Belgian troops back to the English Channel. From May 26 through June 4, a quickly mustered volunteer naval fleet of British fishing boats, pleasure craft, and assorted other vessels staged a heroic evacuation of some 338,000 remaining British, French, and Belgian fighters from Dunkirk, a seaside community in northern France. They left behind a continent that was now firmly in the grip of Nazi Germany.

Great Britain remained the lone nation posing a threat to Germany. In June German submarines, or U-boats, surrounded the British Isles, aiming to cut off shipments of food and other supplies to the British. Hitler hoped to invade Great Britain but knew the British still

A fleet of tiny fishing boats and pleasure craft was able to rescue some 338,000 British, French, and Belgian troops from almost certain annihilation at the French coastal town of Dunkirk. The evacuation commenced on May 27, 1940, and ended nine days later.

The rescue was aided, inexplicably, by an order issued May 24 by Nazi dictator Adolf Hitler, who called off a panzer pursuit of the retreating troops some 20 miles (32 km) from the French coast. Officers of the Luftwaffe had convinced Hitler to let them take over the attack—angering panzer commanders. As German military leaders argued over who should have the honor of finishing off the Allies, the retreating troops were able to shore up their defenses while the rescue fleet sailed across the English Channel. Hitler rescinded the order on May 26, but by then it was too late—the evacuation was about to begin.

Still, the evacuees took heavy fire when the German pursuers finally arrived—some thirty-five hundred troops were killed at sea, while another forty thousand Allied troops were captured before they could board the rescue boats. In London, Winston Churchill—who had replaced Neville Chamberlain as prime minister—called Dunkirk a turning point in the war. In a June 4, 1940, speech made in the British Parliament, Churchill declared, "We shall fight on the beaches, we shall fight on the landing grounds, we shall fight in the fields and in the streets, we shall fight in the hills. We shall never surrender!"

Quoted in James Moore, "The Miracle of Dunkirk: 40 Facts About the Famous Evacuation," *Express* (London), May 21, 2015. www.express.co.uk.

maintained an effective air force. Starting on July 10 Luftwaffe bombers and fighter planes crossed the English Channel to stage raids on British cities. They were met by planes from Great Britain's Royal Air Force (RAF). By October 31 more than eighteen hundred Luftwaffe planes had been shot down over the skies of Great Britain. The RAF sustained heavy losses as well, losing about eleven hundred planes. On the ground, some forty thousand British citizens lost their lives in the Luftwaffe's bombing campaign. Nevertheless, Hitler—fearing that continued air strikes over Great Britain would deplete the Luft-waffe—called a halt to the raids. The air campaign, known as the Battle of Britain, represented the first defeat suffered by German forces since war had been declared a year earlier.

Operation Barbarossa

Throughout 1940 and 1941 skirmishing continued as the war spread elsewhere in Europe and eventually to North Africa. Germany's ally Italy invaded Greece, Egypt, and Libya. Yugoslavia surrendered to the Germans in April 1941. Germany dispatched panzer divisions to North Africa—a significant tank battle was waged between the German and British armies at Tobruk, a port city on the Libyan coast. The battle lasted for 241 days, finally ending in a German victory in 1942.

Following the Battle of Britain, Hitler turned his attention to the east. Despite the pact he had signed with Stalin to invade Poland, Hitler had long despised Stalin and always intended to invade the Soviet Union. "After Stalin's death—he is a very sick man—we will break the Soviet Union," Hitler once boasted. "Then there will be the dawn of the German rule of the earth."[7] To justify his plans to attack the Soviets, Hitler advocated the German concept of *Lebensraum*—literally, "living space"—meaning Germans held the right to push their borders outward to encompass all of Europe. That included conquering the fifteen republics that made up the Soviet Union and enslaving the Slavic people, whom he regarded as inferior. (The Slavs are an ethnic group that makes up the majority of the population of Eastern Europe.) Regarding the Slavs, Hitler said, "As for the ridiculous hundred million Slavs, we will mold the best of them to the shape that suits us, and will isolate the rest of them in their own pigsties; and anyone who talks about cherishing the local inhabitant and civilizing him, goes straight to the concentration camp."[8]

Moreover, the Soviets had embraced communism—an ideology Hitler abhorred. (Under the concept of communism, all national wealth is shared equally by all citizens. In practice, Stalin had centralized governmental control over virtually every aspect of life in the Soviet Union, ruling as a dictator.) Finally, the Soviet Union was home to some 3 million Jews—further evidence, Hitler believed, that Germany must conquer the Soviets as part of his plan to wipe out European Jewry.

On May 22, 1941, Hitler tore up the nonaggression pact he had signed with Stalin and declared war on the Soviet Union. Operation Barbarossa, the German plan to invade the Soviet Union, commenced on June 22, when 3 million German troops, accompanied by three thousand tanks, poured into the Soviet Union. (Barbarossa—meaning "red beard"—was the nickname of the twelfth-century German king Frederick I, who waged many wars throughout the European continent.)

The German troops moved quickly, conquering great swaths of Soviet terrain. At first, they easily overran the Soviet defenders, who did not appear up to the task of fighting off the Germans. Stalin was notoriously suspicious of the Soviet army and for years had purged the ranks of officers whom he suspected of disloyalty. As a result, the army had lost many of its best commanders. By early 1942 the Germans had advanced to the outskirts of Moscow.

But the advance would go no further; the Soviets dug in while the Germans endured a brutally cold Russian winter. Moreover, at

German tanks invade the Soviet Union during the Nazis' Operation Barbarossa in 1941. The Nazi invasion included moving three thousand tanks and 3 million soldiers into the USSR.

the Russian city of Stalingrad, German troops found themselves surrounded by a numerically superior Soviet force. Vicious fighting that lasted from July 1942 through February 1943 ensued on city streets. A third major battle erupted near the city of Kursk, where German and Soviet tanks pummeled each other in July and August 1943. In the end, all three offensives by the Germans had failed. As yet another brutal Russian winter arrived in late 1943, the Germans were forced to pull back and regroup.

Attack on Pearl Harbor

By now the war had grown well past the borders of Europe and engulfed other continents as well. In Asia, Germany's ally Japan intended to establish itself as the dominant force on the continent. By 1941 Japanese troops had invaded China, dominated Korea, and seized islands in close proximity to American-held possessions across the Pacific Ocean. When America responded to Japanese aggression by placing embargoes on shipments of oil, iron ore, and other resources to Japan, the Japanese declared war on the United States. On December 7 Japan staged a surprise attack on the American fleet anchored at Pearl Harbor, Hawaii.

> "Yesterday, December 7, 1941—a date which will live in infamy—the United States of America was suddenly and deliberately attacked by naval and air forces of the Empire of Japan."[9]
>
> —US president Franklin D. Roosevelt

The next day Roosevelt appeared before a joint session of Congress and asked for a declaration of war against Japan. "Yesterday, December 7, 1941—a date which will live in infamy—the United States of America was suddenly and deliberately attacked by naval and air forces of the Empire of Japan,"[9] Roosevelt told members of Congress. Lawmakers quickly passed a declaration of war against Japan. Three days later Congress voted to declare war against Japan's allies, Germany and Italy.

As with France and Great Britain in the wake of Germany's invasion of Poland, the American military was not immediately prepared to respond to the Japanese attack. Indeed, following Pearl Harbor, the Japanese moved quickly, bombing the Philippines, Wake Island, and

Guam—all American possessions. By early 1942 Hong Kong, Indonesia (then known as the Dutch East Indies), Singapore, Myanmar (then known as Burma), and the Solomon Islands had all been invaded by the Japanese.

But later in 1942 the Japanese started suffering setbacks. In June the US Navy defeated Japan at the Battle of Midway Island. In August US Marines landed on Guadalcanal in the Solomon Islands, leading to an Allied victory early the next year. And in September Australian forces engaged the Japanese at Port Moresby, in what is now Papua New Guinea, leading to an Allied victory in early 1943.

The Normandy Invasion

Japan's ally Italy was also losing ground. Following the defeat at Tobruk in 1942, Allied forces in North Africa regrouped and mounted a new offensive, defeating the German panzers in Tunisia in June 1943. Now controlling North Africa, the Allies crossed the Mediterranean Sea a month later, invading the Italian island of Sicily. On July 25 Mussolini was deposed in a coup and held under house arrest.

He was freed by German commandos, who hid him in the town of Gargnano in northern Italy. Mussolini hoped to retake control of his government in Rome, but on September 3 Allied troops landed on the Italian mainland and made their way up the peninsula, entering Rome in June 1944. They were welcomed by cheering Italians who wanted nothing more to do with Mussolini. Italy had now been knocked out of the war.

Mussolini—Hitler's closest ally—was captured by the Italian underground while attempting to flee to Switzerland. On April 28, 1945, Mussolini was executed by the Italian underground—citizens who worked secretly for the Allies—in the town of Mezzegra. His body was hung upside down in a public plaza.

As for the Germans, despite their failure to defeat the Soviets, the Nazi army still dominated much of Europe. Since the launch of Operation Barbarossa, Stalin—now allied with the Western democracies—had appealed to the Americans and British to open a new front against Germany, forcing the Germans to defend eastern and western flanks. By 1944 the Allies were finally ready to open the front, and on June 6 the invasion of France commenced with a landing of more than 150,000

troops from twelve Allied nations along the coast of Normandy, France. They represented the first wave of more than 4.5 million Allied troops who now made their way toward Berlin.

Germany Surrenders

Although the Normandy invasion was widely successful, the Allies faced one final challenge from the German army in December 1944 and January 1945 when the Germans launched a panzer attack in the Ardennes Forest in Belgium. It is known as the Battle of the Bulge because the Germans marshaled some 250,000 troops and one thousand panzer tanks in an effort to break through the Allied lines. But the offensive failed, forcing the Germans to retreat.

By April Hitler was hiding in a bunker below the streets of Berlin. Overhead, Soviet troops had advanced into Berlin, wiping out what little resistance remained while they searched for the Nazi leader. Hitler feared capture by the Soviets. He knew they would execute him but only after subjecting him to a humiliating trial in Moscow.

On April 30 Hitler married his longtime mistress, Eva Braun. Following the ceremony, Hitler and Braun retreated to the privacy of their chambers, where they committed suicide. On May 7, 1945, Germany formally surrendered to the Allies.

Flight of the *Enola Gay*

But Germany's ally Japan continued to fight on. Now ejected from many of the territories they controlled throughout the Pacific, the Japanese found themselves facing Allied navies that been closing in on the Japanese mainland for months. In a final, desperate strategy, Japanese aircraft carriers dispatched their pilots to attack enemy vessels. Encased in the noses of their planes were bombs designed to detonate on contact. For the pilots these were suicide missions, because to detonate the bombs they had to crash their planes into the

Hiroshima, Japan, was devastated by an atomic bomb dropped by US forces on the city on August 6, 1945. After another A-bomb was dropped on the city of Nagasaki three days later, the Japanese surrendered, ending World War II.

enemy ships. In Japan a pilot in one of these missions was known as a kamikaze—literally, "divine wind."

Moreover, Allied commanders were convinced the Japanese would never surrender and that even civilians would take part in the defense of the Japanese mainland. Military planners estimated an invasion of Japan would require 2.5 million Allied troops, and the Allies could expect to suffer losses of 1 million or more. US president Harry S. Truman—who took office after Roosevelt's death on April 12, 1945— decided that was too high a price to pay in the lives of American and Allied soldiers. So Truman authorized the use of a new weapon that had been secretly under development in America since the early days of the war. The weapon—the atomic bomb—is capable of mass destruction. The bomb causes massive devastation by splitting an atom, unleashing enormous destructive energy.

On August 6 the US Army bomber *Enola Gay* dropped an atomic bomb on the Japanese city of Hiroshima. Three days later a second atomic bomb was dropped on the city of Nagasaki. The bombs all but obliterated the two cities and took the lives of some 106,000 people. On August 14, 1945, Japan surrendered.

The world had never seen a conflict as destructive as World War II. The people of Germany, Japan, and Italy put their trust in authoritarian dictators who dreamed of world domination and the enslavement of the conquered. These dreams were shattered over the course of six devastating years by others who lived under much higher ideals.

CHAPTER TWO

How Did the Treaty of Versailles Lead to the Rise of the Nazis?

Focus Questions

1. Do you think the terms of the Treaty of Versailles were too harsh on the German people? Why or why not?
2. Could Germany have taken steps to avoid hyperinflation and economic disaster after the war? Explain your answer.
3. What are some of the factors that led to the popularity of the Nazi Party in post–World War I Germany—and why?

During the turmoil in Germany following the end of World War I, the country's new leadership enacted a new constitution. After centuries of servitude to a monarchy, the German people suddenly found themselves living under a constitution modeled after the body of laws found in America and the other Western democracies. Adopted in the German city of Weimar in 1919, the constitution provided for a government administered by a chief executive—the chancellor—whose duties were similar to those of the American president. A bicameral legislature known as the Reichstag, similar to the US Congress, enacted new laws. Citizens were promised free speech, the right to assembly, and other freedoms. Women were given the right to vote—a full year before the US Constitution was amended to grant suffrage to women.

The authors of the German constitution sought to provide the population with the tools to rebuild their society, but this promise could not stand up to the bitterness that gripped the German people in the years after the war. When German troops marched home following the end of hostilities in France, they did not regard themselves as a vanquished army. Indeed, during the course of the war no enemy troops had ever invaded German soil. Rather, the German people believed they had been the victims of cowardly and duplicitous leaders who had lost the will to fight.

Moreover, the terms of the treaty German leaders were forced to sign to end the war—the Treaty of Versailles—were extremely harsh. If followed to the letter, they would subject the German people to decades of hunger and poverty while leaving open the possibility that Germany could not defend itself against its hostile neighbors. The Treaty of Versailles, meant to bring peace to Europe, instead served only to undermine the new German democracy, providing the basis of the extremist views of Adolf Hitler and the Nazi Party, which grew to dominate German society.

The Great War

World War I—then known as the Great War—was in its time the most devastating conflict to have afflicted the civilized world. Over the course of four years of combat, more than 37 million soldiers and civilians from multiple countries lost their lives. The war had many causes. Among them was a tradition dating back to medieval times: European kings attempted to exert their dominance over the Continent by sending their armies to invade their neighbors. These actions ended in disaster for those monarchs, among them Kaiser Wilhelm II, who had ruled Germany since 1888. He abdicated during the final days of the war.

Wilhelm's abdication was announced on November 9, 1918. Two days later the Allies declared a cessation of hostilities against Germany. The German troops withdrew from France, where most of the fighting had occurred, and marched home convinced their leaders had betrayed them. It was a notion shared by the families and friends they rejoined.

In January 1919 Allied leaders gathered in Paris to negotiate a treaty. Among the delegates were the American president, Woodrow Wilson, as well as David Lloyd George, the prime minister of Great Britain; Georges Clemenceau, prime minister of France; and Vittorio Orlando, prime minister of Italy, which had fought on the side of the Allies in World War I.

This painting documents the signing of the peace treaty at Versailles in Paris, France, in 1918, ending World War I. The victorious Allies did not include the defeated Germans in the treaty negotiations, but instead dictated to them the treaty's terms.

Significantly, leaders of Germany's new democratic government were not invited to attend—suggesting that instead of negotiating a treaty with Germany, the Allied leaders intended to dictate terms to the Germans. Indeed, in late 1918, shortly before the Paris talks got under way, Eric Geddes, a British political leader, proclaimed in a speech, "We will squeeze Germany like a lemon. We will squeeze her until you can hear the pips squeak."[10] In fact, German representatives were not summoned to the peace talks until May—after the terms of the treaty had already been decided by the Allies.

The War Guilt Clause

At the peace conference, the French joined the British in arguing for punitive damages against Germany. The majority of the war had been fought on French soil, Clemenceau declared, and his country now had to rebuild farms, industries, villages, and cities that had been ravaged during four years of combat. Wilson agreed with the French and British leaders who sought harsh reparations against the Germans. "I have always detested Germany," Wilson confided to Lloyd George. "I have never gone there. But I have read many German books on law. They are so far from our views that they have inspired in me a feeling of aversion."[11]

Under the terms of the treaty, Germany was forced to cede the Alsace-Lorraine region to France, which it had seized from the French following an 1871 war. Germany was also forced to give up territory to Poland and Belgium. The Germans were ordered to disarm, reducing their army to a force of just 100,000 troops (down from 11 million troops that had seen battle during the war). Moreover, the German military was ordered to scrap its airplanes and submarines, as well as most of its surface ships. Clearly, the Allies intended to remove all capability for the Germans to pose a threat to the security of Europe.

From the Germans' perspective, the most punishing demand in the treaty was the financial obligation the Allies placed on their country to repay them for the cost of the war. The demand for reparations followed Article 231 of the treaty, known as the war guilt clause. Article 231 read, "The Allied and Associated Governments affirm and Germany accepts the responsibility of Germany and her allies for causing all the loss and damage to which the Allied and Associated Governments and their nationals have been subjected as a consequence of the war imposed upon them by the aggression of Germany and her allies."[12]

> "May the hand wither that signs this treaty."[13]
>
> —Philipp Scheidemann, German chancellor

Throughout the four years of the conflict, the German people never considered themselves the aggressors. Over the course of the war, Germans had been told their troops fought valiantly in defense of the empire. And when hostilities ended, they believed the German troops marched home not in defeat, but with their honor intact. German chancellor Philipp Scheidemann declared, "May the hand wither that signs this treaty."[13]

Occupation of the Ruhr

The financial requirements of the treaty were as stringent as the other terms. The Allies set the debt at $32 billion. In today's dollars $32 billion is a formidable amount of money. In 1919 it was a truly staggering amount. The Allies also forced Germany to accept a French military occupation of the Ruhr region until the debt was repaid. The Ruhr, in western Germany, is a heavily industrialized region housing most of the country's steel and coal production. Indeed, in the event the German government missed payments of reparations to the French, the French troops intended to seize coal, steel, and other goods and send them back to France.

> "As a soldier I cannot help feeling that it were better to perish honorably than to accept a disgraceful peace."[14]
>
> —Paul von Hindenburg, German general

Back in Germany, government officials fretted over the terms and delayed approval of the treaty. On June 16 the Allies notified the Germans they had until June 24 to approve the terms; failure to act by the deadline would mean resumption of hostilities—in other words, an invasion of Germany, carried out by the French.

German leaders wondered whether that would be their best option—to mount a military resistance against the treaty. They discussed rearming and using German troops to block the French from entering the Ruhr. Paul von Hindenburg, the general who led the German military during much of World War I, counseled against raising an army against the French. "We can scarcely count upon being able to withstand a serious offensive on the part of the enemy in view of the numerical superiority of the [French] and their ability to outflank us on both wings," Hindenburg told German leaders on June 17. "The success of the operation as a whole is therefore very doubtful, but as a soldier I cannot help feeling that it were better to perish honorably than to accept a disgraceful peace."[14]

German leaders heeded Hindenburg's advice. On June 24 the German legislature approved the treaty. Four days later delegates representing the victorious and vanquished nations assembled in the Palace of Versailles, about 12 miles (20 km) from Paris, to sign the Treaty of Versailles.

Runaway Inflation

The effects of the treaty were felt immediately throughout Germany. Even before the war ended, the German economy was suffering. To pay for the tremendous cost of equipping an army and waging war across the European continent, the German government had taken out massive loans from German banks. As the war dragged on, depleting the German treasury, Wilhelm resisted his ministers' advice to repay the loans by raising taxes on the German people. Instead, Wilhelm's government made payments on the debt by simply printing more money—a tactic that backfired. Germany experienced runaway inflation, meaning prices were rising even as the purchasing power of currency was falling.

German children in 1923 use German paper money as building blocks during playtime. Runaway inflation following World War I had made the country's currency worthless.

By the end of the war, German marks (the name of the country's currency) were all but worthless. Germans found they literally needed wheelbarrows full of marks to buy milk, eggs, bread, soap, clothing, shoes, and other necessities of life. "My father was a lawyer," recalled Walter Levy, a New Yorker who was born in Germany, "and he had taken out an insurance policy in 1903, and every month he had made the payments faithfully. It was a 20-year policy, and when it came due, he cashed it in and bought a single loaf of bread."[15] Inflation was so bad that even thieves did not bother with German marks. In 1923 a *New York Times* reporter interviewed Max Weisse, a German who was robbed of his cash on a Berlin street. When he turned over his wallet, the robber found some American and British cash as well as German marks. The robber gave the marks back to Weisse. "Thank you; we don't bother ourselves with those anymore,"[16] the robber told Weisse.

In November 1923 the value of German money had fallen so low that economists declared a single US dollar was worth 1 *trillion* German marks. But that did not stop the German government from continuing to print worthless money to pay the war reparations demanded under the Treaty of Versailles. Knowing the German marks were without value, the French protested and in 1923, under the terms of the treaty, sent troops into Germany to occupy the Ruhr. French troops seized German coal and shipped it back to France. German coal miners responded by going on strike. Violence erupted in several Ruhr cities.

Elsewhere in Germany, chaos reigned as well. American author Pearl S. Buck, traveling through Germany, wrote:

> The cities were still there, the houses not yet bombed and in ruins, but the victims were millions of people. They had lost their fortunes, their savings; they were dazed and inflation-shocked and did not understand how it had happened to them and who the foe was who had defeated them. Yet they had lost their self-assurance, their feeling that they themselves could be the masters of their own lives if only they worked hard enough; and lost, too, were the old values of morals, of ethics, of decency.[17]

The National Socialists

Watching all this chaos unfold was a movement of German extremists known as the National Socialist German Workers' Party—in German, *Nationalsozialistische deutsche Arbeiterpartei*, abbreviated as Nazis. The Nazis were led by Hitler, a veteran of the Great War. The Nazis harbored a number of beliefs that at first alienated them from mainstream German society, but as conditions continued to erode in their country, the German people embraced Hitler and the Nazis as saviors who could rebuild their economy and empower the Germans to forge a powerful nation.

Birth of the Nazi Party

Anton Drexler, a Munich locksmith, founded the Nazi Party in 1919, originally calling it the German Workers' Party. It was one of many extremist organizations that formed in Germany following adoption of the Treaty of Versailles and the disintegration of the German economy.

Early meetings of the party drew just a handful of followers. In September 1919 Adolf Hitler attended a meeting. Hitler, a German army veteran of World War I, remained in the military following the war—it was one of the few places where Germans could find steady employment. Assigned to a unit investigating subversive organizations, Hitler found himself agreeing with the rhetoric he heard voiced at the meeting: extreme nationalism, German exceptionalism, racial purity, anti-Semitism, and anticommunism. These views represented the components of what Hitler would later call National Socialism. Hitler joined the party, quit the army, and devoted himself full-time to building the German Workers' Party into a formidable political organization.

As German society fell into chaos, the German Workers' Party gained members—within a year thousands were attending its rallies. In 1920, under Hitler's urging, party leaders changed the name to the National Socialist German Workers' Party—abbreviated as the Nazi Party. As for Drexler, in 1921 Hitler engineered a coup to oust the locksmith as party leader. Drexler remained a nominal member but never again enjoyed a measure of authority in the Nazi Party. He died in 1942.

The Nazis held a number of racist notions, mainly that the Aryan race of blue-eyed, blond-haired Germanic people was the "master race"—superior physically and intellectually to all others. "All human culture, all the results of art, science, and technology that we see before us today, are almost exclusively the creative product of the Aryan,"[18] Hitler declared in his book *Mein Kampf* (*My Struggle*), which he published in 1925. Moreover, the Nazis harbored deep prejudices against many ethnic groups—particularly Jews. The Nazis blamed Jewish leaders in the German government for the collapse of the German army in the waning months of the war and also blamed Jewish bankers for the hyperinflation that gripped German society. Other ethnic groups were also targeted. Hitler despised blacks and Roma—then known as gypsies. Hitler found gays repulsive. He also believed it was his mission to enslave the Slavic people by invading and conquering the Soviet Union—thus fulfilling his vision of *Lebensraum*.

> "All human culture, all the results of art, science, and technology that we see before us today, are almost exclusively the creative product of the Aryan."[18]
>
> —Adolf Hitler

At first Hitler and the Nazis were regarded as fanatics. On November 8, 1923, Hitler led a Nazi insurrection in the city of Munich, where they attempted to overthrow the Bavarian state government. The plot was foiled by German troops. Hitler was convicted of treason and sentenced to five years in prison—ultimately serving just eight months.

Path to a Second War

The months he spent in prison did not change Hitler's intentions. He still aimed to take over the German government but had learned his lesson in Munich. He now knew that armed insurrection would not be a successful path. Instead, Hitler spent the next decade spreading the Nazi message, and as conditions continued to deteriorate in Germany, his words found traction among the destitute German people.

Indeed, in 1928 Nazi candidates won just 2 percent of the seats in the Reichstag. A year later the German economy was thrown into

Assassination of Walther Rathenau

As the German economy declined in the aftermath of the Treaty of Versailles, much of the wrath by extremists fell on Walther Rathenau. As minister of reconstruction and later foreign minister in the democratic Weimar government, Rathenau was charged with overseeing the repayment of war reparations to the Allies.

Although life was harsh in postwar Germany, Rathenau did achieve a diplomatic victory that eased some of the burden on the German people. In 1922 he negotiated the Treaty of Rapallo, in which the Soviet Union agreed not to seek reparations from Germany. (The Soviet Union was established in the aftermath of World War I; however, Russia, now a Soviet republic, had fought on the side of the Allies.) But Rathenau was Jewish, which made him the focus of anti-Semitic rhetoric promoted by extremist critics.

Rathenau was aware of his unpopularity. He once confided to his friend, the German physicist Albert Einstein, "My heart is heavy. . . . A man alone—knowing his limits and weaknesses—what can a man like that do in this paralyzed world, with enemies all around?"

On June 24, 1922, Rathenau's car was cut off by an automobile carrying three men. Two men got out; one man, armed with a submachine gun, fired into Rathenau's car. A second man tossed a hand grenade into the car. Members of an extremist group known as Organization Consul took credit for the assassination. The assassins were caught—one was killed by police, one committed suicide, and the third was sentenced to a prison term of seven years. Eventually, Organization Consul disbanded as its members joined the Nazi Party.

Quoted in Rochelle L. Millen, ed., *New Perspectives on the Holocaust: A Guide for Teachers and Scholars*. New York: New York University Press, 1996. p. 54.

further turmoil after the collapse of the US stock market. The collapse led to worldwide economic depression, which hit the German economy particularly hard. In fact, before the stock market collapse, the German economy was recovering from the chaos caused by the

Treaty of Versailles. In 1924—in response to the invasion of the Ruhr—American banker Charles G. Dawes worked out a plan to restructure Germany's debt, giving the country more time to repay its war reparations. Moreover, American bankers agreed to loan Germany $200 million to help pay its war debts and rebuild its economy.

Adolf Hitler was elected as chancellor of Germany in 1933. This position allowed him to move forward with his plan to make Germany the ruler of the world.

But after the stock market crash, American aid to Germany dried up, and the Germans once again faced economic catastrophe. The Germans responded by accepting Hitler's desire to rebuild Germany by conquering its enemies. In the 1930 elections, Nazi candidates won 18 percent of the seats in the Reichstag; two years later the Nazis won 37 percent of the seats, making the Nazis the largest party in the Reichstag. On January 30, 1933, Hitler was named chancellor of Germany.

Soon Hitler commenced his plan to rebuild Germany into the most powerful nation in Europe. His most immediate act was to ignore the terms of the Treaty of Versailles. War reparation payments ceased. Moreover, the treaty's requirement that the German military consist of no more than one hundred thousand troops was ignored. Within five years of Hitler's ascendancy to the chancellorship, Germany exercised its might by annexing Austria and seizing the Sudetenland. The path to a second war, which arguably started in the Palace of Versailles nineteen years earlier, was now clear.

CHAPTER THREE

How Did Japanese Militarism Lead to the War in the Pacific?

Focus Questions

1. How might a stronger response by the United States to the Tripartite Pact have influenced the Japanese decision to attack Pearl Harbor?
2. Do you believe the Japanese were justified in their hostility toward Americans over US immigration policy? Why or why not?
3. How much responsibility did the isolationists in Congress bear for the attack on Pearl Harbor? Explain your answer.

Japanese civilization is believed to date back some six thousand years, but for most of its history Japan remained an isolated society. In 1853 Japan was coaxed out of its isolationism by US Navy commodore Matthew Perry, who offered a treaty to open trade with Japan. Within a few decades Japan transformed itself from an isolated and agrarian culture into an industrialized society carrying on trade all over the world. As Japan built its industries, it also built a formidable military, charged with the mission of ensuring that no nation would stand in the way of Japan's lust for wealth.

In the years following Perry's visit, the Japanese realized they lacked the raw materials to build a competitive industrial society. Raw materials such as coal, oil, and iron ore were vital to the country's economic growth. Japan was forced to import most of its raw materials in order to supply the factories and manufacture the goods that would make it into an economic powerhouse of Asia. Says economist Robert Higgs, "In the late nineteenth century, Japan's economy began to grow and to industrialize rapidly. Because Japan has few natural resources, many of the burgeoning industries had to rely on imported raw materials, such as coal, iron ore or steel scrap, tin, copper, bauxite, rubber, and petroleum."[19]

What raw materials Japan could not get through trade it obtained by force. On more than one occasion, Japanese leaders sent the military to neighboring countries to seize lands rich in the raw materials needed to feed the Japanese industrial machine. In 1894 Japan used its troops to expel the Chinese army from Korea. With the Chinese gone from Korea, Japan helped itself to the abundant sources of coal and iron ore available in the country. Moreover, under the treaty that ended that conflict with China, Japan won ownership of the island of Formosa (now known as Taiwan), where the Japanese tapped the island's reserves of coal, oil, gold, and sulfur, a chemical used in the manufacture of fertilizer. The Japanese also seized a huge swath of Chinese territory known as Manchuria, where they found abundant reserves of coal, iron, and oil. Manchurian farmers grew soybeans and tobacco, which the Japanese seized as well. A decade later Japan waged war against Russia, quickly and decisively defeating the European power. As a result of the Russo-Japanese War, Japan seized further territory in Manchuria, which had been controlled by Russia.

Japan's Aggressive Foreign Policy

Despite Japanese aggression throughout Asia, the Americans and Japanese maintained robust relations. It was, for example, President Theodore Roosevelt who brokered the treaty that ended the Russo-Japanese War. And the United States had emerged as Japan's most important trading partner. Among the Japanese products purchased by American consumers were silk and other textiles, pottery, furniture, bicycle parts, electric appliances, paper, cement, rubber boots, and toys. But by the 1920s the long-standing goodwill between the United States and Japan started showing signs of strain.

America's attitude toward Japanese immigrants was partly to blame. Japan's explosive economic growth had also resulted in a population explosion, and by the dawn of the twentieth century, the Japanese were grappling with the problems of overpopulation, such as housing and food shortages. One of their solutions was to encourage Japanese citizens to immigrate to America. But this was an era when America's labor unions were growing in influence, and they did not

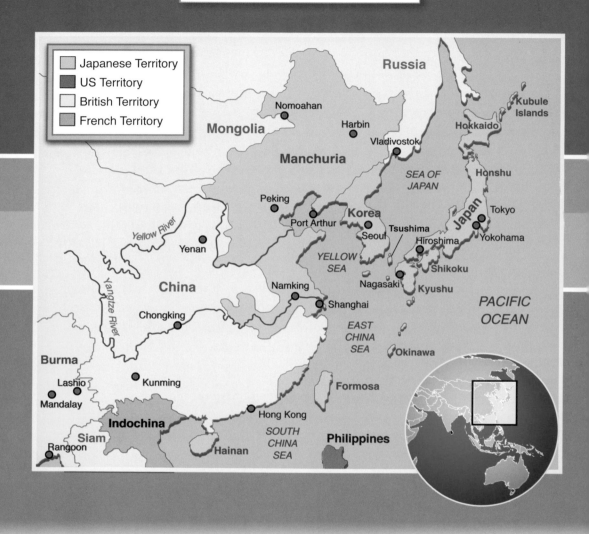

Japanese Expansion 1895–1938

Legend:
- Japanese Territory
- US Territory
- British Territory
- French Territory

Russia
Mongolia
Manchuria
Nomoahan
Harbin
Vladivostok
Kubule Islands
Hokkaido
SEA OF JAPAN
Honshu
Peking
Port Arthur
Korea
Seoul
Tsushima
Hiroshima
Tokyo
Yokohama
Japan
Yellow River
Yenan
YELLOW SEA
Shikoku
China
Namking
Nagasaki
Kyushu
PACIFIC OCEAN
Shanghai
Chongking
Yangtze River
EAST CHINA SEA
Okinawa
Burma
Lashio
Kunming
Formosa
Mandalay
Hong Kong
Indochina
SOUTH CHINA SEA
Philippines
Siam
Rangoon
Hainan

welcome immigrants from Asia who offered to work for wages far below what American unions were demanding for their members. Under pressure from American labor leaders, the US government slowed Japanese immigration to America.

In 1926 the emperor Hirohito ascended to the throne of Japan. Hirohito is believed to have taken little interest in his government's foreign policies, leaving the strategizing to his ministers. And over the next fifteen years, Hirohito's government came to be dominated by ministers with military backgrounds, who believed that Japan's superior army and navy should be employed to carry out the nation's foreign policy.

The influence of Hirohito's militaristic ministers surfaced on July 7, 1937, when open warfare erupted between Japanese and Chinese troops when a Chinese patrol boat opened fire on Japanese troops at the Marco Polo Bridge near the Chinese capital of Beijing. By this time Japanese troops had moved beyond the borders of Manchuria and had now surrounded Beijing, just a few miles south of Manchuria. The Japanese claimed the troops' mission was to protect cargo aboard railway cars moving between the Chinese capital and Japanese-held territory in Manchuria, but with Japanese troops surrounding the capital, tensions were high. Chinese officials suspected Japan had intentions to move beyond the borders of Manchuria and dominate the entire nation.

The Japanese responded to the incident at the Marco Polo Bridge by sending additional troops from Manchuria into northern China. The Japanese navy formed a blockade of China along the coastline, cutting off China's access to the Pacific Ocean. By 1938 Japan controlled most of China, although Chinese guerrillas would carry on the fight against the Japanese for years to come. Japanese aggression continued into 1939 as the Japanese army occupied Hainan Island off the coast of China, as well as the strategically important Spratlys—islands with airstrips that could be used to attack targets, including French Indochina and the Philippines. Both of these had abundant raw materials coveted by the Japanese for their country's industrial growth needs.

Menace to Japan

Even before the 1937 war between China and Japan, the US government had voiced its opposition to Japanese aggression but took little action to deter the Japanese from continuing their policy of conquering their neighbors. In 1932 Secretary of War Henry Stimson issued the Stimson Doctrine, declaring that the United States recognized China's independence. When the Japanese invaded the country five years later, however, the American government did little to help the Chinese—merely offering a token loan of $25 million to assist the

Chinese government. By then, signs of war were growing in Europe, and the US Congress was dominated by isolationists who did not want to see America drawn into another foreign war—in Europe or Asia.

Still, the US government did take some steps to protect America's interests in the Pacific. For decades, as Japan made aggressive moves throughout Asia, the United States was also expanding its influence in the Pacific. Following the Spanish-American War in 1898, the American government gained dominion over the former Spanish colonies of the Philippines and Guam. Hawaii, then still a territory, was also under American control. Among the other Pacific islands under control of the American government were Wake Island, Midway Island, and American Samoa.

Japanese troops muster at a railway station in Manchuria, a section of northeastern China that the Japanese forcibly annexed. In 1937 continued Japanese aggression erupted in war with China.

To protect these possessions, in 1940 the US Navy moved its Pacific Fleet from its base in San Diego, California, to Pearl Harbor on the Hawaiian island of Oahu. The Japanese regarded the fleet's move to Pearl Harbor as a threat. Indeed, the American fleet was now anchored just some 3,800 miles (6,116 km) from the Japanese mainland—a distance that could be crossed by American warships in just a few days. Says historian Gordon W. Prange, "The United States Navy . . . [threatened] Japan's path—a navy which Japanese admirals thought capable of menacing their nation's very existence."[20]

The US government took other measures to send a message to Japan that further aggression would not be tolerated. In July 1940 Franklin D. Roosevelt ordered an embargo on shipments of raw materials to Japan—mainly scrap iron and steel. Tensions between Japan and the United States were now very high and were further stoked by events that unfolded thousands of miles away. In September 1939 the European war erupted after Germany's invasion of Poland. The following June, France fell to the German army—setting the stage for Japan's next major aggressive move, an action that ultimately led Japan into war against America.

> "The United States Navy . . . [threatened] Japan's path—a navy which Japanese admirals thought capable of menacing their nation's very existence."[20]
>
> —Gordon W. Prange, historian

The Tripartite Pact

With France now dominated by German occupiers, Japan saw an opportunity to take control of French Indochina—a region that now encompasses the nations of Vietnam, Laos, and Cambodia. In September 1940 Japan's powerful army easily overran a token force of local defenders, seizing control of the French colony after just three days. Five days after the invasion, Japan signed the Tripartite Pact with Germany and Italy, allying it with the two European dictatorships.

The Tripartite Pact effectively backed the United States into a diplomatic corner. To move militarily against Japan's aggression in the Pacific meant attacking an ally of Germany and Italy, which would mean entering the war in Europe—a prospect the isolationists in Congress still staunchly opposed. However, to continue trading with the Japanese meant doing business with an ally of Germany and Italy—now fighting a war against Great Britain, which was receiving shipments of arms and other supplies from America to continue the war against the Germans. Moreover, the Japanese made it clear they planned to continue their aggression until they dominated the entire Asian continent. Said Japan's premier, Fumimaro Konoe, "Asia is absolutely necessary to the continued interest of this country."[21]

> "Asia is absolutely necessary to the continued interest of this country."[21]
>
> —Fumimaro Konoe, Japanese premier

America's ambassador to Japan, Joseph Grew, was well aware of Japanese intentions. He considered his government's failure to move against Japan in response to the invasion of French Indochina similar to Great Britain's policy of appeasement toward Nazi Germany during the Sudetenland crisis. Grew wrote in his diary on January 1, 1941:

> With all our desire to keep America out of war and at peace with all nations, especially with Japan, it would be the height of folly to allow ourselves to be lulled into a feeling of false security. . . . Japan, not we, is on a warpath. . . . If those Americans who counsel appeasement could read even a few of the articles by leading Japanese in the current Japanese magazines wherein their real desires and intentions are given expression, our peace-minded fellow countrymen would realize the utter hopelessness of a policy of appeasement.[22]

Crippling Economic Embargoes

In Washington, Roosevelt spent eleven months mulling over the US response to the Japanese invasion of French Indochina. Finally, on July 26, 1941, Roosevelt ordered a freeze on Japanese assets, including Japanese money deposited in American banks. This meant that Japanese depositors no longer had access to their wealth in America. On August 1 Roosevelt enacted the most crippling economic embargo on Japan, cutting off oil exports to the Japanese. At the time of the embargo, Japan had been relying on America for 88 percent of its oil supply.

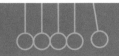

As the victorious Japanese planes arrived back at their carriers after the attack on Pearl Harbor, Japanese admiral Isoroku Yamamoto (who had planned the Pearl Harbor attack) is said to have turned to other officers and uttered these words: "I fear we have awakened a sleeping giant and filled him with a terrible resolve." In the years since the attack, historians have concluded that many leaders of the Japanese government and military knew prior to the attack that their country would never be able to win a protracted war against the American military. However, Japanese leaders were well aware that the US Congress was dominated by isolationists who wanted to keep America out of a global war, and they hoped these isolationists would negotiate rather than fight. Says historian David M. Kennedy:

> The plan was hugely ambitious but not mad. Its slender logic resided for the most part in the hope that the isolationist and militarily unprepared Americans would be so stunned by Japan's lightning blows that they would lose the will to fight a protracted war, and would accept a negotiated settlement guaranteeing Japan a free hand in Asia. All the Japanese planners understood that a conventional victory, ending in the complete defeat of the United States, was an impossibility.

Quoted in Crosby Day, "Yamamoto's 'Sleeping Giant' Quote Awakens a Gigantic Argument," *Orlando (FL) Sun-Sentinel*, October 28, 2001. http:/articles.sun-sentinel.com.

Quoted in *Atlantic*, "Nobody Expects the Japanese Invasion: How Pearl Harbor Blindsided America," December 7, 2012. www.theatlantic.com.

By now Japan had for months been preparing for war against the United States. Military strategists focused on Pearl Harbor, knowing they had to cripple the American fleet if they hoped to control what would inevitably become the Pacific theater of war.

Still, there were some diplomatic measures taken to avoid war. In January 1941 Japan dispatched Kichisaburo Nomura to Washington to negotiate a resolution to the disputes between the United States and Japan. Although a retired admiral, Nomura was not considered by the Americans to be an advocate of war against the United States. Therefore, American diplomats believed Japan was sincere in wanting to resolve its differences with the United States and would be open to America's demands that Japan withdraw from French Indochina and China. Nevertheless, upon his arrival, Nomura engaged in long and ultimately fruitless negotiations with American diplomats.

Nomura's efforts to seek peace were reined in by the new Japanese prime minister, Hideki Tojo. A Japanese army general, Tojo had been appointed minister of war in 1940—a position he used to oversee Japan's preparation for war against the United States. He was named prime minister in October 1941.

> "The Japanese proposal on November 20 . . . was of so preposterous a character that no responsible American official could ever have dreamed of accepting it."[23]
>
> —Cordell Hull, US secretary of state

On November 20 Nomura presented US secretary of state Cordell Hull with a new set of terms to settle the crisis. In exchange for the end of the embargoes of oil and other goods and lifting the freeze on Japanese assets, Japan promised to withdraw troops from southern Indochina—but would continue to maintain a military presence in northern Indochina. As for its domination of China and other Asian countries, Japan had nothing to say. Japan also remained silent on the subject of the Philippines, Guam, and other American territories. Finally, the communication to Hull made no mention of Japan's intentions regarding whatever Japan had promised its European allies—Germany and Italy. Following the war, in 1946 Hull testified before members of Congress, "The Japanese proposal on November 20 . . . was of so preposterous a character that no responsible American official could ever have dreamed of accepting it."[23]

The Minutes Tick Away

Still, Hull did not immediately dismiss the Japanese offer. He told Nomura the US government would take the offer under advisement. But after conferring with Roosevelt, on November 26 Hull delivered the US response: It renewed America's desire to continue the embargoes until Japan withdrew its troops from China and French Indochina. On the day Hull issued his response, a Japanese naval task force—including five aircraft carriers—weighed anchor from a port in the Kurile Islands north of Japan and steamed for Hawaii.

On Saturday, December 6, Japanese foreign minister Shigenori Togo notified Nomura that Japan intended to present a new fourteen-point message to the Americans and that the message was to be delivered precisely at 1:00 p.m. Washington time, the next day. Contained in the message was a declaration of war, with hostilities to commence one hour after the message was delivered. At the time the message

The Element of Surprise

Japanese military planners knew an attack on Pearl Harbor could succeed only if they caught the Americans by surprise. And so, prior to the December 7, 1941, attack, the Japanese engaged in a game of deception. A week before the planned attack, the Japanese stepped up naval activity near Malaya (now known as Malaysia), about 6,700 miles (10,783 km) from Hawaii. American military observers in the region reported the activity to US Navy headquarters in Washington, DC, where officers concluded the Japanese fleet posed no immediate threat to Pearl Harbor. Missing from the activity near Malaya, though, were the Japanese aircraft carriers. They were already steaming toward Hawaii.

The attack was timed to commence on a Sunday morning. The Japanese knew that many Americans attend church services on Sunday mornings and presumed, correctly, that few Americans would be on duty defending Pearl Harbor against an attack. Moreover, the weather favored the Japanese. On December 5 and 6, as the Japanese fleet neared Hawaii, low clouds covered the Japanese ships—shielding them from view by American reconnaissance planes flying overhead.

When Japanese bombers swooped down on Pearl Harbor just before 8:00 a.m. on December 7, they were able to take full advantage of the element of surprise. Says Robert J. Hanyok, a former US Department of Defense intelligence analyst, "Of all the aspects of the attack on that . . . Sunday morning—including its treachery, swiftness, daring, and skillful execution—none seems more compelling than the assault's total surprise."

Robert J. Hanyok, "How the Japanese Did It," *Navy History*, December 2009. www.usni.org.

was to be delivered, Japanese warplanes were already to have departed from their carriers and be flying toward Hawaii.

But the transmission of the message was delayed. It arrived at the Japanese embassy in bits and pieces. As Japanese diplomats worked through Sunday morning piecing the message together for presentation to Hull, the minutes ticked away and the planes drew closer to Hawaii. In fact, the ultimatum was finally delivered at 2:05 p.m. By that time, the Japanese attack was already under way.

Long Siege Ahead

The planes arrived over Pearl Harbor at 7:55 a.m.—or just before 2:00 p.m. Washington time—on December 7. Although there had been radar sightings of the approaching planes, commanders on the ground misinterpreted the signals and chose to ignore them. Meanwhile, at 6:45 a.m.—more than two hours before the Japanese planes arrived—the USS *Ward*, a Navy destroyer on patrol, spotted a small Japanese submarine attempting to slip into Pearl Harbor. The *Ward* sank the submarine and reported the incident, but again, navy headquarters took no action.

And so when the Japanese planes arrived, they found the navy base defenseless and unprepared for the attack. In the space of just 110 minutes, Japanese forces damaged or destroyed sixteen American warships anchored in the harbor, as well as nearly three hundred military aircraft parked in hangars or along runways at nearby Hickam Field and other air bases on the island. More than twenty-four hundred Americans, including sixty-eight civilians, were killed in the attack. Another twelve hundred Americans were wounded.

Back in Washington, by the time Hull received the fourteen-point message from the Japanese, he had already been notified that the attack on Pearl Harbor had commenced. The communication essentially relisted the many complaints the Japanese harbored against the United States, concluding with this statement: "The Japanese Government regrets to have to notify hereby the American Government that in view of the attitude of the American Government it cannot but consider that it is impossible to reach an agreement through further negotiations."[24]

At 2:20 p.m. Hull summoned the Japanese ambassador into his office. He told Nomura, "In all my 50 years of public service I have never seen a document that was more crowded with infamous falsehoods and distortions—infamous falsehoods and distortions on a scale so

The USS *Arizona* burns in Pearl Harbor, Hawaii, after a Japanese surprise air attack on December 7, 1941. The attack pulled the United States into World War II.

huge that I never imagined until today that any Government on this planet was capable of uttering them."[25] The next day Congress voted to authorize the war.

On December 11 the Germans honored their commitment to the Tripartite Pact by declaring war on the United States. Adolf Hitler had not been apprised by the Japanese of their plans to attack Pearl Harbor but was nevertheless delighted by Japan's aggression against America. Hitler had long feared America's entry into the war, which would mean that German soldiers would face US troops. Now that Japan had attacked the United States, Hitler believed the Americans would concentrate their forces in the Pacific and pose no immediate threat to the German army in Europe.

Hitler was wrong. Although the United States certainly did have to mobilize against the Japanese, by June 1942 fifty thousand American soldiers and sailors had arrived in Great Britain to prepare for the war against Germany. They were among the first wave of 2.4 million American troops eventually dispatched to Europe to engage the Germans in the long siege ahead. And in the Pacific, the Japanese found themselves facing some 2.8 million American troops by the end of the war.

CHAPTER FOUR

How Did the Normandy Invasion Lead to Germany's Surrender?

Focus Questions

1. Why do you think the Germans failed to predict the consequences of a two-front war?
2. Why do you think Adolf Hitler ignored his generals' pleas to seek a peace treaty with the Allies?
3. What factors were most important to the success of the Normandy invasion and why?

The war in Europe had been raging for more than four years when the leaders of the three major Allied powers—US president Franklin D. Roosevelt, British prime minister Winston Churchill, and Soviet leader Joseph Stalin—attended a summit to decide the future course of the conflict. By now the German army was well entrenched across the European continent. Although Allied troops had landed on the Italian mainland in September 1943 when they entered the southern coastal province of Salerno, their progress north through the Italian peninsula was slow. In fact, by November 1943 the Allied advance had essentially stalled at the Mignano Gap, a narrow mountain pass some 100 miles (161 km) southwest of Rome.

On the eastern front, the Nazi drive into the Soviet Union stalled due to the cold Russian winters as well as dogged Soviet troops. Nevertheless, by the summer of 1943 some 4 million German troops were still deployed in the Soviet Union. Indeed, Stalin's troops were suffering tremendous casualties while the Germans continued their occupation of great swaths of the Soviet Union. To turn the tide against the Germans,

Allied leaders knew they would have to open a second front in Europe. In fact, as early as 1942 Allied military leaders recognized the need to open a western front—to land an invasion force in France, forcing the Germans to confront an advancing army in the west while maintaining the war against the Soviets in the east. Says historian Denys Schur:

> It can be said that the "Second Front" issue had been the pivotal question in building Allied strategy from the time the anti-Hitler coalition was created till the very moment of the invasion. . . . The opening of the Second Front in Northern Europe deprived the Germans of any chance of revival. There was no longer any hope for the Nazi leaders, not counting Hitler's maniacal belief in final victory, that Germany would be able to prevail over numerically and materially superior adversaries while fighting a two-front war.[26]

The Tehran Conference

But such a plan was not seriously discussed until November 28, 1943, when the three Allied leaders met in Tehran, Iran, to plan the second front. Over the course of the four-day Tehran Conference, Roosevelt, Churchill, and Stalin developed a strategy, code-named Operation Overlord, which entailed transporting tens of thousands of Allied troops across the English Channel and landing them along the coast of France. The Allies would then sweep across France and Belgium, pushing enemy troops back to Germany.

"The opening of the Second Front in Northern Europe deprived the Germans of any chance of revival."[26]

—Denys Schur, historian

Meanwhile, Stalin agreed to stage a new offensive, preventing the Germans from transferring troops from the eastern front to France. Roosevelt, Churchill, and Stalin scheduled Operation Overlord to commence in May 1944. At the conclusion of the Tehran Conference, the three Allied leaders issued this statement:

> No power on earth can prevent our destroying the German armies by land, their U-boats by sea, and their war plants from the air.

Our attack will be relentless and increasing.

Emerging from these cordial conferences we look with confidence to the day when all peoples of the world may live free lives, untouched by tyranny, and according to their varying desires and their own consciences.

We came here with hope and determination. We leave here, friends in fact, in spirit and in purpose.[27]

Assault on Five Beaches

Many months before the Tehran Conference, the Allies commenced a massive troop buildup, and by early 1944 some 3.5 million Allied troops were camped in Great Britain, awaiting orders for the invasion. Meanwhile, in January 1944 US Army general Dwight D. Eisenhower assumed command of Allied troops in Europe and ordered final plans drawn up for Operation Overlord.

Military planners targeted the invasion for five beaches near the French town of Caen in a region of France known as Normandy. The landing site was selected because of the nature of the terrain beyond the beaches—the fields and pastures would provide easy access for the Allied troops to the French interior. Units of the British and Canadian militaries would land at beaches code-named Gold, Sword, and Juno. The Americans would assault the beaches code-named Omaha and Utah. More than just an amphibious landing, the invasion would consist of bombardments of German positions by navy ships, bomber strikes over the Normandy coastline, commandos flown in by gliders, and paratroopers dropped behind enemy lines. D-day, as the invasion came to be known, was set for May 1.

As May 1 approached, though, Eisenhower decided the troops needed more time to prepare. He rescheduled the assault for the first

> "No power on earth can prevent our destroying the German armies by land, their U-boats by sea, and their war plants from the air. Our attack will be relentless and increasing."[27]
>
> —Joint statement by US president Franklin D. Roosevelt, British prime minister Winston Churchill, and Soviet leader Joseph Stalin

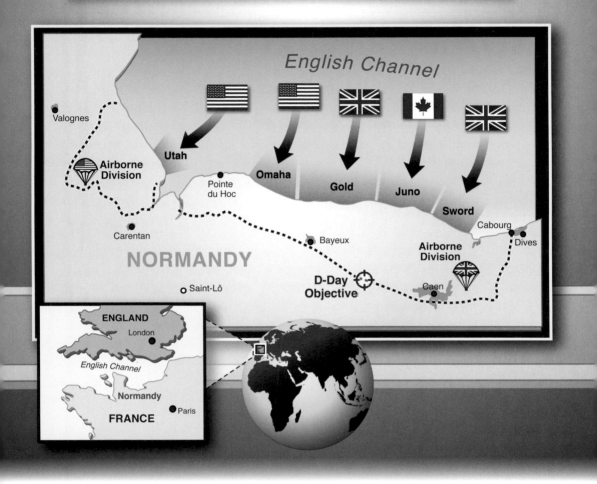

week of June. On the night of June 3, Eisenhower convened a meeting of military chiefs. Nearby, 150,000 troops had already boarded vessels in British harbors and were awaiting orders to make the overnight journey to the French coast. Moreover, 10,500 military planes stationed at British air bases awaited orders to take off. All plans had now been finalized, awaiting Eisenhower's order to commence the invasion. But as Eisenhower learned at the June 3 meeting, the weather was not cooperating.

Storms had swept through the region. The cloud cover over the Normandy coastline was too dense, meaning the bombers would not be able to find their targets below. Without sufficient air cover, Eisenhower feared the beach assault would fail. If the storms persisted for

America's Two-Front War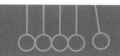

As with Germany, America was forced to fight a two-front war during much of World War II. One front was the known as the European theater of operations and included the Allied invasions of Italy and France. The other front was staged across the Pacific Ocean against Japan in what was known as the Pacific War. Unlike Germany, America was able to sustain a two-front war because of its massive availability of raw materials, such as coal, oil, and steel, as well as its resources of troops available for service in the armed forces. More than 16 million Americans served in the army, navy, marines, and coast guard during World War II. In contrast, Germany was forced to fight a two-front war with some 11 million members of its military.

Following the victory over Germany in 1945, the Allies prepared for the invasion of Japan. During the summer of 1945, the US military began transferring troops to the South Pacific, stationing them on the island of Okinawa, which is about 970 miles (1,561 km) south of Tokyo. Okinawa was to have been the staging ground for the planned invasion of Japan. But on July 16, after scientists successfully detonated an atomic bomb in the desert near Alamogordo, New Mexico, President Harry S. Truman made the decision to use the bomb against the Japanese rather than suffer the losses of 1 million Allied troops expected to fall in the invasion.

several days, it could mean the invasion would be delayed for weeks—the landing craft needed low tide in order to make the beach assault. Low tide was necessary because the Germans had fortified the beaches by planting obstructions such as tree stumps in the sand—designed to smash into troop transports as they entered shallow water. Low tide would expose the obstructions. For the invasion the tide was most favorable on June 5, 6, and 7. Planners concluded the tide would not be favorable again for weeks.

Fooling the Germans

A lengthy delay in the invasion could have devastating effects because the Allies hoped to catch the Germans by surprise. In fact, German military chiefs were well aware the Allies were planning an invasion, but they disagreed on the time and place. The Germans expected the invasion to take place in May and were mystified as to why Eisenhower let the favorable weather that dominated most of the month go to waste. On May 30 Field Marshal Gerd von Rundstedt, who commanded all German military operations in western Europe, reported to Hitler that he did not believe an invasion was imminent.

Moreover, Rundstedt, as well as another key general, Field Marshal Erwin Rommel, commander of the defenders along the French coastline, were convinced that when the invasion was finally ordered, it would most likely occur near the town of Calais, where the English Channel was at its narrowest. Indeed, by crossing the channel to Calais, the invasion force would have to cross a mere 27 miles (43 km) of sea. (The distance between the British coast and the Normandy beaches was 118 miles, or 190 km.) Therefore, the Germans concentrated most of their forces on defending the beaches near Calais, 157 miles (253 km) north of the actual invasion site at Normandy.

The Allies encouraged this notion among the Germans by feeding them false intelligence. In a maneuver known as Operation Fortitude, as D-day neared the Allies sent out phony radar images suggesting a massive fleet was approaching the French coast near Calais.

By delaying the invasion for weeks, the Allies feared the Germans would eventually see through the ruse and rush their troops to Normandy. So at the June 3 meeting, Eisenhower decided that before calling off the invasion, he would wait one more day.

The Invasion Begins

On the night of June 4, meteorologist James M. Stagg, a captain in the RAF, was summoned to make a report on the weather. The storms, Stagg said, were expected to continue for a number of days. However, Stagg predicted a temporary break in the weather, starting the afternoon of June 5 and lasting until the afternoon of June 6. Skies over Normandy would be clear during that window. After hearing Stagg make his report, Eisenhower smiled and said, "OK, we'll go."[28]

The invasion began quietly, just after 1:00 a.m. on June 6, when British and American paratroopers dropped out of the sky near Caen. German sentries reported the arrival of the Allied troops, but their commanders were slow to react. In fact, Rundstedt was awakened and told of the paratroop assault, but he refused to believe it was the first wave of a major invasion. He ordered no mass mobilization of German defenses.

At dawn on June 6, the waters off the coast of Normandy suddenly filled with Allied ships—some five thousand vessels in all. Seconds after the ships emerged from the mist, the sky was filled with thundering booms as the ships blasted the shoreline with artillery shells. Overhead, the skies filled with planes bombing enemy positions. Below, the German defenders could do little but hide behind concrete bunkers.

The first troops landed on Utah Beach at 6:31 a.m., when their amphibious carriers entered shallow waters, dropped their ramps, and discharged their soldiers. They encountered little resistance—due largely to the naval and air bombardments. The troops moved quickly ashore.

Allied troops land at Omaha Beach in Normandy on D-day, June 6, 1944. The Omaha Beach landing met stiff German resistance and incurred many casualties.

The troops landing at Omaha Beach encountered much stiffer resistance. German machine guns opened fire as soon as the Americans left their landing crafts. Moreover, the beach was heavily mined—killing many troops as they stepped on explosive devices planted in the sand. And the naval and air bombardments had failed to wipe out most of the German positions. S.L.A. Marshall, a US Army officer who participated in the invasion, later described the landing at Omaha Beach:

Already the sea runs red. Even among some of the lightly wounded who jumped into shallow water the hits prove fatal. Knocked down by a bullet in the arm or weakened by fear and shock, they are unable to rise again and are drowned by the onrushing tide. Other wounded men drag themselves ashore and, on finding the sands, lie quiet from total exhaustion, only to be overtaken and killed by the water. A few move safely through the bullet swarm to the beach, then find that they cannot hold there. They return to the water to use it for body cover. Faces turned upward, so that their nostrils are out of water, they creep toward the land at the same rate as the tide.[29]

Peril Beyond the Beach

All morning, landing craft continued to discharge American troops onto Omaha Beach, where they found themselves pinned down by German fire. American ships stepped up their bombardment of the German positions, and by 11:00 a.m. the battle finally turned in favor of the Americans. On the beach, commanders pressed their men to rise and attack. "Two kinds of people are staying on this beach," shouted Colonel George A. Taylor to his troops, "the dead and those who are going to die. Now let's get the hell out of here!"[30] A major breakthrough occurred when US Army Rangers scaled a 100-foot (30-m) cliff overlooking the beach and knocked out German batteries raining fire down on the beach below.

> "Two kinds of people are staying on this beach, the dead and those who are going to die."[30]
>
> —US Army colonel George A. Taylor

At Gold, Juno, and Sword Beaches, the British and Canadians faced less opposition than the Americans at Omaha Beach. The naval and aerial bombardments had helped soften the German defenses, but for the British troops arriving at Sword Beach the peril awaited inland. The Germans dispatched their lone panzer division in the vicinity to the territory just beyond Sword Beach, stationing the tanks between the Allied invaders and the town of Caen. Just as the two armies prepared to clash, the skies suddenly filled with British aircraft, disgorging thousands of paratroopers. Within minutes, British troop strength had doubled. Seeing his panzer division was now greatly outnumbered, General Edgar Feuchtinger called off the attack.

By the end of the day, the Allies had successfully landed more than 150,000 troops on the French coast. They were followed by millions more who soon made their way to Germany.

Urged to Negotiate Peace

Operation Overlord accomplished its goal: to squeeze the German army between two advancing enemies—the Western Allies in the west and the Soviets in the east. Nobody knew the harsh consequences of the Normandy invasion more than Hitler's generals. Within days of the invasion, the Allied armies had advanced well into France and were easily overrunning spotty German resistance.

On June 17 Hitler's two key generals on the western front, Rundstedt and Rommel, met with the dictator to advise him that the German army could not withstand the Allied onslaught. A third general, Hans Speidel, attended the meeting. Later, he wrote:

> "[Hitler] sat hunched upon a stool, while the field marshals stood. His hypnotic powers seemed to have waned."[31]
>
> —German general Hans Speidel

[Hitler] looked pale and sleepless, playing nervously with his glasses. . . . He sat hunched upon a stool, while the field marshals stood. His hypnotic powers seemed to have waned. There was a curt and frosty greeting from him. Then in a loud voice he spoke bitterly of his displeasure at the success of the Allied landings, for which he tried to hold the field commanders responsible.[31]

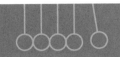

Following the Normandy invasion, high-ranking members of the German military became convinced the war was not winnable. They appealed to Adolf Hitler to seek a negotiated peace with the Allies. Hitler refused.

Therefore, these members of the military hatched a plan to assassinate Hitler and seize control of the German government. Among the conspirators was Field Marshal Erwin Rommel. On July 15, 1944, Rommel made a final effort to convince Hitler to order a retreat. He sent a telegram to the dictator warning Hitler that the German military could not stop the advancing Allied armies in France. "I gave him his last chance," Rommel told an aide. "If he does not draw the consequences, we will have to act." Rommel did not get a chance to participate in the conspiracy. On July 17 he was severely wounded when his car was struck by fire from a British fighter plane.

Three days later Colonel Claus von Stauffenberg entered a conference room near Rastenburg, Germany, where Hitler had convened a meeting of military leaders. Stauffenberg left a briefcase in the meeting, then walked out. Moments later, a bomb in the briefcase exploded. But Hitler survived the plot, sustaining only minor burns.

Hitler ordered the roundup and execution of the conspirators. Nearly five thousand German soldiers and civilians are believed to have been executed, including Stauffenberg. As for Rommel, he was eventually discovered to have participated in the plot. He committed suicide on October 14, 1944, rather than face arrest and execution.

Quoted in Klaus P. Fischer, *Nazi Germany: A New History*. New York: Continuum, 2003, p. 551.

Rommel told Hitler that a new Soviet offensive was sure to commence soon on the eastern front. Rommel urged Hitler to order a retreat of all troops back to Germany and seek a negotiated end of the war with the Allies. "Don't you worry about the future course of the war, but rather about your own invasion front," Hitler snapped back at Rommel. General Alfred Jodl, who also attended the meeting, said later, "Hitler paid no attention whatsoever to their warnings."[32]

Defeated German troops are marched through Moscow in 1944. Hitler's tactical error allowed the Soviets to overcome invading Nazi troops, leading to the eventual surrender of Germany.

Germany Surrenders

As Rommel predicted, the Soviet offense began soon after his meeting with Hitler. At 5:00 a.m. on June 22, the Soviets commenced a massive artillery bombardment along the German-Soviet front in the Soviet republic of Belarus, which borders Poland to the east. As with the Normandy invasion, the Germans guessed wrong about where the Soviet offensive would be launched. Hitler was convinced the offensive would be staged further south, targeting Hungary, Romania, and Bulgaria—countries he believed Stalin wished to annex into the Soviet Union. Therefore, the German military concentrated its forces in that region, some 400 miles (644 km) from the action.

Germany's much-feared panzer corps was easily overwhelmed. Near the Belarus city of Vitebsk, the Soviets encircled a panzer corps under the command of German general Friedrich Gollwitzer, who was forced to surrender. Some thirty-five thousand German troops were taken prisoner, including Gollwitzer. Later, a German sergeant recalled the battle: "No one knew what was going on. There were Russians behind us, to the right and to the left. We fired. My God, but it was useless. It was like firing at the ocean waves with the tide coming in."[33] In mid-August 1944 the first Soviet troops crossed onto German soil and were now just 350 miles (563 km) from Berlin.

Meanwhile, on the western front, the Allied armies easily swept through France. The French city of Cherbourg was liberated on June 27; on July 18 the Germans were ousted from the city of Saint-Lô. Paris was liberated on August 25. The Allies moved next into neighboring Belgium. By September 4 the Germans had been ousted from the Belgian cities of Brussels and Antwerp. The Western Allies and the Soviets were now moving from two different directions toward Berlin.

For Hitler the end came on April 30, 1945, when he committed suicide as Soviet troops overran the streets of Berlin. Germany officially surrendered on May 7.

The invasion of Normandy set in motion the concerted effort of the Allied nations to bring World War II to a close. Prior to the morning of June 6, 1944, the Allies lacked the troop strength to overcome the German war machine, which had spent the previous five years dominating the European continent, digging in and fortifying its positions. In the end, though, the German army was unable to maintain a two-front war as both sides closed in on Hitler, trapping him in his bunker below the streets of Berlin.

CHAPTER FIVE

How Did the Marshall Plan Revitalize Postwar Europe?

Focus Questions

1. If the Allies had established a European aid program following World War I, do you think there would have been a second world war? Explain your answer.
2. Do you believe there is a direct link between the Soviet Union's refusal to accept Marshall Plan aid and the country's collapse forty-three years later? Why or why not?
3. How do you think America benefits from a unified European continent?

In the weeks following the Nazi surrender, Allied troops made their way through Germany, as well as the European countries that had been occupied by the German military. They found widespread destruction: homes, factories and businesses leveled by months of aerial bombing or street-by-street fighting. Food was scarce—virtually everyone was hungry. Hospitals overflowed with the wounded.

Philip Dark, a lieutenant in the British army, recalled arriving in the German city of Hamburg just days after the Nazi surrender:

> We . . . enter a city devastated beyond all comprehension . . . . It was more than appalling. As far as the eye could see, square mile after square mile of empty shells of buildings with twisted girders scarecrowed in the air, radiators of an [apartment] jutting out from a shaft of a still-standing wall, like a crucified pterodactyl skeleton. Horrible, hideous shapes of chimneys sprouting from the frame of a wall. The whole pervaded by an atmosphere of ageless quiet. . . . Such impressions are incomprehensible unless seen.[34]

In the aftermath of the war, nearly 20 million Germans were believed to be homeless. Half the civilian population of the cities of Berlin, Hanover, and Hamburg had been killed during the war, mostly by Allied bombing. In the city of Cologne, the civilian death toll was believed to be as high as 70 percent.

The Nazi-occupied countries also suffered terrible devastation. Moreover, this destruction was not due solely to Allied bombing. In 1943 a large section of Warsaw, Poland, was burned to the ground by the Nazis to flush out rebellious Jews who had staged a two-year armed resistance against German occupiers. A year later Adolf Hitler ordered the remainder of Warsaw razed as Polish rebels armed themselves and mounted a new resistance. By the time they were through, Nazi occupiers had destroyed more than 90 percent of the dwellings in Warsaw.

The German port city of Hamburg was reduced to smoldering ruins by Allied bombing in World War II. Half the city's population died in the war, a scene that was repeated in other major German cities as well.

Rural communities were similarly destroyed. Farms were burned, plundered of their crops, or simply neglected. In the Netherlands, retreating German troops opened the dikes, flooding 500,000 acres (202,343 ha) of farmland. As the Western Allies and Soviet troops liberated countries and advanced toward Berlin, the ruthless Nazi leader Heinrich Himmler declared, "Not one person, no cattle, no quintal of grain, no railway track must remain behind. . . . The enemy must find a country totally burned and destroyed."[35]

> "The enemy must find a country totally burned and destroyed."[35]
>
> —Heinrich Himmler, Nazi leader

Commitment by the American People

As Allied leaders surveyed the destruction of the European continent in the aftermath of the German surrender, they were faced with the daunting task of feeding millions of starving Europeans, building new homes for them, and rebuilding their economies. The task of rebuilding Europe fell to George C. Marshall, a former US Army general who was appointed secretary of state by Harry S. Truman in January 1947. To develop what was officially known as the European Recovery Program, Marshall appointed William L. Clayton, a former executive of a cotton trading company, and George Kennan, a longtime US Department of State diplomat. Others instrumental in writing the plan were Arthur H. Vandenberg, an influential US senator from Michigan, as well as US Department of State diplomat Dean Acheson and W. Averell Harriman, the US secretary of commerce. The aid program—familiarly known as the Marshall Plan—was launched in 1948. Over the course of four years, the program provided some $13 billion (an amount equal to $129 billion in today's dollars) in cash as well as food and other goods to European countries to help them rebuild homes, businesses, and infrastructure; feed their citizens; and revive their agriculture.

The plan represented a substantial commitment on the part of the American people. After all, the war years had been difficult for them as well. Throughout the war, Americans found themselves living on ration cards, limiting the amount of food they could buy. In 1948, $13 billion represented roughly 3 percent of the annual production of the American economy. A few months before the plan was unveiled,

Marshall delivered a speech at Harvard University in Massachusetts in which he emphasized the importance of rebuilding Europe: "The truth of the matter is that Europe's requirements for the next three or four years of foreign food and other essential products—principally from America—are so much greater than her present ability to pay that she must have substantial additional help, or face economic, social and political deterioration of a very grave character."[36]

Communists and Chaos

The Foreign Assistance Act of 1948—the law adopted by Congress to implement the Marshall Plan—set up an agency to oversee how the aid would be distributed to Europe. That agency, known as the Economic Cooperation Administration (ECA), was charged with reviewing the needs of each country and developing strategies to deliver the aid. The ECA was also charged with setting up channels of trade between American suppliers and European customers—in other words, finding companies in America willing to sell goods to the Europeans, as well as identifying the proper European customers for those goods. Moreover, the ECA guaranteed payment for the goods sold to the Europeans with money appropriated by Congress.

Certainly, Truman, Marshall, and other American leaders felt they had to help rebuild Europe on humanitarian grounds, but there were other reasons to aid the Europeans as well. American industries—and therefore American workers—would have been substantially affected if European customers lacked the ability to buy American goods. Indeed, prior to the war some 70 percent of all American food exports were delivered to European countries. Said US secretary of agriculture Clinton Anderson, "Unless the economy of that area can be restored to a strong, self-supporting basis, the producers of our export crops will suffer directly, and our farmers will suffer indirectly."[37]

American political leaders were also concerned about Soviet intentions in Europe. Stalin had already made moves toward gaining dominance over eastern Europe. US leaders worried that failure to rebuild the devastated nations could leave room for Communist movements to rise amid the chaos and eventual alliances with Stalin's government in Moscow. In April 1947, as the Marshall Plan was still being developed, Clayton warned Marshall, "Europe is steadily deteriorating.

Millions of people in the cities are starving. If things get any worse, there will be revolution."[38]

The Hand of Stalin

Stalin's plans for control of Eastern Europe began to take shape shortly after the war had ended. Three months after the Nazi surrender, Stalin, Truman, and Churchill met in the German city of Potsdam to decide how they would administer Germany. The American, British, and Soviet leaders elected to split Germany into four zones, with each country administering one zone and France administering the fourth. The Potsdam Agreement specified that each country was to use its resources to begin rebuilding the German economy, eliminate the last remnants of Nazism in the vanquished country, bring war criminals to justice, and prepare Germany for a democratic government.

Splitting Germany into zones was seen as a temporary measure. Publicly, the Allies declared their intention to eventually turn the administration of Germany over to a democratically elected government administered by German political leaders. But Truman and Churchill suspected Stalin's true plan was to establish a Communist regime in Germany and install his hand-picked representatives to administer the government.

> "Europe is steadily deteriorating. Millions of people in the cities are starving. If things get any worse, there will be revolution."[38]
>
> —William L. Clayton, architect of the Marshall Plan

On June 7, 1948, representatives of the British, American, and French governments met in London and announced an agreement to unite the three German zones into an autonomous country, to be known as the Federal Republic of Germany (or West Germany). The Soviets refused to permit the zone under their command to join; in 1949 they declared the Soviet zone the autonomous country of the German Democratic Republic (or East Germany). The German Democratic Republic would be administered by a Communist regime, friendly to the Soviets, for the next four decades.

Meanwhile, Stalin's hand could be seen elsewhere. In January 1946 a Communist government assumed power in Albania, a country in eastern Europe. In January 1947 Communists seized power in Poland.

Operation Vittles

Joseph Stalin's hostility toward the Marshall Plan erupted into a confrontation against America in 1948 when the Soviet leader enacted a blockade of the city of Berlin. By starving Berliners and causing chaos, Stalin hoped to clear the way for the takeover of the city government by German Communists.

At the time the city of Berlin, located in the Soviet zone, was itself split into four zones, each respectively administered by the Americans, British, French, and Soviets. The confrontation erupted after German Communists protested plans by the Americans to introduce a new currency—the deutsche mark—into Berlin. American officials said a common currency used throughout Germany was needed to facilitate the purchase of goods by German consumers. The Soviets instead proposed their own currency for the Soviet zone, the *ostmark*.

On June 24 the Soviets announced a blockade of the city. Soviet troops surrounded Berlin. Roads were blocked. No trains were permitted to enter Berlin. Electrical power was cut off. Inside the city's three free zones, there was just enough food to feed the 2.3 million Berliners for a month.

America and Great Britain responded by organizing an airlift of military planes, flying into the Berlin free zones to deliver food. The Berlin Airlift—codenamed Operation Vittles—lasted into 1949. America and Great Britain ultimately flew 2.3 million tons (2 million metric tons) of food and other supplies into Berlin— until Stalin halted the blockade.

Within a few years Communist regimes were also established in Romania, Hungary, Bulgaria, Czechoslovakia, and Yugoslavia, forming what was known as the Eastern Bloc. Over the next four decades, these states were largely ruled by totalitarian regimes allied closely with the Soviet Union.

No Longer Enemies

As the specter of Soviet domination over Europe grew, American leaders desperately wanted to maintain democratic governments in Western Europe—a goal that was aided in no small measure by the Marshall Plan. During the four years of the program, the Marshall Plan distributed cash, food, raw materials, tools, and other products to Austria, Belgium, Denmark, France, Great Britain, Greece, Iceland, Ireland, Italy, Luxembourg, the Netherlands, Norway, Portugal, Sweden, Switzerland, Turkey, and West Germany.

West Germany was earmarked for aid under the Marshall Plan despite objections from French officials, whose country had suffered terribly under the Nazi occupation. As they did following World War I, French officials favored reparations imposed on the German people. Moreover, French officials sought to establish their country as Europe's predominant industrial powerhouse and feared that if Germany was able to rebuild, German industries would compete with French corporations for the economic dominance of the Continent. This time, however, the Americans did not agree. They had no wish to repeat history by causing runaway inflation in the German economy, upheaval in the German government, and the likelihood that Germany would be taken over by a hostile regime—in this case a puppet government controlled by the Soviet Union. Says historian John Gimbel, "[The United States] became more critical of France's aims and objections regarding Germany and the future of Europe, and it finally concluded that France's territorial and economic demands were, in fact, incompatible with any program that would have Germany achieve a viable economy in the future."[39]

The story of the German automaker Volkswagen illustrates the success of the Marshall Plan. Before the war, in an era when cars were too expensive for most people, Hitler had envisioned a vehicle that average Germans could afford. Hitler had even provided preliminary sketches for the car, known as the Volkswagen. A factory was erected in the town of Wolfsburg and production commenced, but few cars were actually made because the factory was soon retooled to produce military vehicles.

The factory was bombed and heavily damaged during the war. Following the war the British army assigned a military engineer, Ivan Hurst, to reopen the factory so it could be used to repair British military vehicles used in the occupation of Germany. While repairing the factory Hurst discovered the plans for the Volkswagen and appealed to his superiors to produce the tiny car as a way of employing workers in a country suffering from widespread unemployment. The British government agreed, and in a few short months production of Volkswagen cars began again.

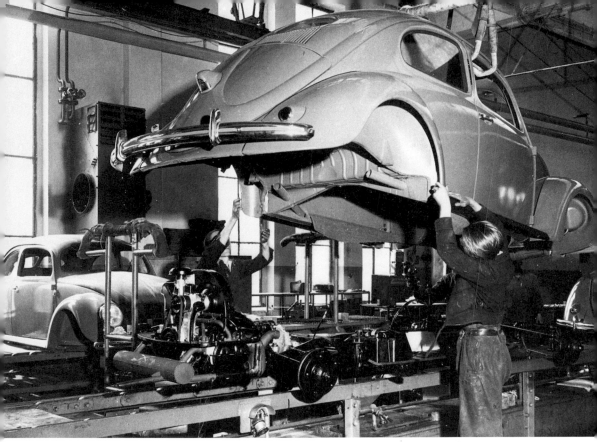

A Volkswagen Beetle is constructed at the original factory in Wolfsburg, West Germany, in 1949. Damaged in Allied bombing raids, the factory was restored by the British so Germans could find work after the war.

Although Hurst got the Wolfsburg plant up and running, it was initially hampered by the lack of machinery needed to produce the car's components. By 1949 Hurst had turned over operation of the factory to Heinrich Nordhoff, a former executive with the German car company Opel. To overcome the factory's deficiencies, Nordhoff was awarded nearly $750,000 through the Marshall Plan. Nordhoff used the money to buy American-made production machines, which were shipped to Wolfsburg and installed in the Volkswagen factory. Author Andrea Hiott points out that in enabling Nordhoff to buy the parts, the Marshall Plan not only helped Volkswagen produce cars, it also greatly aided the American companies that sold production machines to the German car company. She says, "The [Volkswagen] plant also benefited greatly from the new attitude the Marshall Plan helped to instill: In Europe and America, it was becoming possible to think of Germany in a way other than 'the enemy' again."[40]

Today Volkswagen sells cars all over the world. In 2015 the company sold some 10 million vehicles under the brands of Volkswagen, Porsche, Audi, and others. The company operates 130 plants in thirty-one countries. Arguably, none of it would have been possible if postwar leaders had not seen the importance of rebuilding Europe.

> "In Europe and America, it was becoming possible to think of Germany in a way other than 'the enemy' again."[40]
>
> —Andrea Hiott, author

The Marshall Plan also paid for Europeans to travel to America to learn new techniques in how to do business. Says economist William James Adams, "Under the Marshall Plan, France dispatched large numbers of business executives, trade unionists, [and] civil servants to the United States with an eye toward absorption of American productivity. They returned not only with . . . butch haircuts and wineless lunches, but also with an appreciation of how business was conducted."[41]

European Cooperation

As companies like Volkswagen grew and trade channels were opened by the ECA throughout the Continent, the European nations found it in their interest to cooperate both economically and politically. This was a far different attitude than had been held by European leaders in decades past. Indeed, jealousy and ambition harbored by European kings led them to make war on one another for generations, culminating finally in World War I. And in the aftermath of that war, the Nazis in Germany and Fascists in Italy had rebuilt their nations not in the spirit of cooperation with neighboring countries but with the goal of conquering their neighbors.

But in the years following World War II, European leaders were guided largely by the spirit of the Marshall Plan. They elected to work together, forging their economies through free trade among themselves. Their ultimate goal was to enhance the wealth of their citizens. Henry Kissinger, who served as US secretary of state under presidents Richard Nixon and Gerald Ford, suggests that this spirit of cooperation led European leaders to agree to the creation of the North Atlantic Treaty Organization (NATO), as well as the European Union

(EU). NATO—formed in 1949 by European and American leaders—is a military alliance in which member nations agree to act as one against aggression. In other words, an attack against one member of NATO is considered an attack against all members.

The EU, formed in 1993, is a coalition of nations that has sought to create a common economy among all members. In addition to creating a common currency—the euro—under the EU agreement, regulations regarding trade, tariffs, travel, and immigration are standardized among all members, fostering a spirit of cooperation rather than competition. Indeed, in 2017 *Forbes* magazine reported that four of the richest countries in the world—in terms of average annual income per worker—were recipients of Marshall Plan assistance: Luxembourg, Norway, Switzerland, and the Netherlands. "In Europe, the Marshall Plan helped consolidate nations whose political legitimacy had evolved over centuries," says Kissinger. "Once stabilized, those nations could move on to designing a more inclusive, cooperative order."[42]

A scene from downtown Oslo, the capital city of Norway, is shown. Norway, a post–World War II Marshall Plan recipient, is now one of the world's wealthiest nations.

Collapse of the Soviet Union

However, many countries turned down Marshall Plan aid—specifically, the countries under the Soviet umbrella as well as the Soviet Union itself, which suffered terribly during the Nazi invasion. Czechoslovakia had actually accepted an invitation to a meeting of diplomats to

Long Lines in Moscow

The Soviet Union and Eastern Bloc countries were not served well by their decision to turn down Marshall Plan aid or by their embrace of communism over capitalism. While French business leaders learned how to organize factories and Italian handbag makers gained access to American leather suppliers, the Soviets and their Eastern Bloc allies collectivized farms, meaning they combined thousands of family-owned farms into huge, government-run establishments. Collectivization eliminated the farmers' profit motive and therefore the desire to work hard. A 1989 US Library of Congress study found that by 1953—the year of Stalin's death—farms in the Soviet Union produced less food than they produced in the 1920s. In contrast, by 1951 countries that had received Marshall Plan aid were producing 11 percent more food than they produced in 1938.

And so the economies of the Soviet Union and Eastern Bloc nations largely stumbled along for the next four decades. By the 1980s residents of Moscow were forced to wait in long lines for hours to buy food, clothes, and other household necessities. Visiting a Moscow grocery store in 1982, *New York Times* correspondent John F. Burns reported:

> On weekend days, a visitor to food shops in Moscow can see lines of buses chartered by residents of towns 50 and 100 miles away. Women wearing headscarves and felt boots fill cardboard suitcases and knapsacks with as much meat and produce as they can buy. Recently a woman buying more than what others considered her fair share snapped that she had traveled seven hours through a snowstorm.

John F. Burns, "Soviet Food Shortages: Grumbling and Excuses," *New York Times*, January 15, 1982. www.nytimes.com.

discuss the plan; when Stalin learned of the meeting he summoned Czechoslovakian foreign minister Jan Masaryk to Moscow and forbade him from accepting Marshall Plan aid.

Instead, the Soviets relied on their Communist ideology to propel their economy as well as the economies of the Eastern Bloc nations. Over the decades, the Soviets and Eastern Bloc nations found themselves increasingly unable to compete in world markets. Their technology was backward, Soviet workers had no incentive to work hard, and corruption was rife in business and government. Moreover, in 1981 Leonid Brezhnev, the leader of the Soviet Union, was forced to publicly concede that Soviet agriculture was incapable of providing enough food to feed the country's 267 million people. In contrast, France has emerged as the European continent's leading food producer—a circumstance created in no small part by the fact that Marshall Plan aid helped deliver twenty-five thousand new tractors to French farmers in the years following World War II.

In 1991 the Soviet Union—beset by decades of internal dissent as well as economic ills—finally collapsed. Many of the former Soviet republics as well as the Eastern Bloc nations embraced democracy, opened trade with the West, and worked toward modernizing their economies. The two Germanys united into a democratic state. Today eleven members of the twenty-eight-nation EU are either former Soviet republics or former members of the Eastern Bloc.

The Marshall Plan proved to be an enormously successful component of American foreign policy in the late 1940s and early 1950s. It helped rebuild much of Europe, marginalized the Soviets, and helped bring Germany back into the community of nations. It was a far different expression of foreign policy than that which had been embraced by the Western Allies following World War I when the Treaty of Versailles led to chaos, discontent, the rise of the Nazis, and ultimately a second world war.

Introduction: Appeasement at Munich

1. Quoted in William L. Shirer, *The Rise and Fall of the Third Reich*. New York: Simon & Schuster, 1960, p. 403.
2. Quoted in Shirer, *The Rise and Fall of the Third Reich*, p. 391.
3. Quoted in International Churchill Society, "The Munich Agreement: October 5, 1938, House of Commons," 2016. www.winstonchurchill.org.
4. Shirer, *The Rise and Fall of the Third Reich*, p. 364.

Chapter One: A Brief History of World War II

5. Stephen E. Ambrose and Cyrus Leo Sulzberger, *American Heritage History of World War II*. Boston: New Word City, 2015. Kindle edition.
6. Quoted in Klaus P. Fischer, *Nazi Germany: A New History*. New York: Continuum, 2003, p. 439.
7. Quoted in Fischer, *Nazi Germany*, p. 439.
8. Quoted in Shirer, *The Rise and Fall of the Third Reich*, p. 951.
9. Quoted in Digital History, "Pearl Harbor Speech: Day of Infamy," University of Houston, 2016. www.digitalhistory.uh.edu.

Chapter Two: How Did the Treaty of Versailles Lead to the Rise of the Nazis?

10. Quoted in Martin Pugh, *Hurrah for the Blackshirts: Fascists and Fascism in Britain Between the Wars*. London: Pimlico, 2006, p. 75.
11. Quoted in Manfred F. Boemeke, Gerald D. Feldman, and Elisabeth Glaser, eds., *The Treaty of Versailles: A Reassessment After 75 Years*. Cambridge: Cambridge University Press, 1998, p. 603.
12. "Peace Treaty of Versailles," Brigham Young University Library, 1998. http://net.lib.byu.edu.
13. Quoted in Shirer, *The Rise and Fall of the Third Reich*, p. 57.
14. Quoted in Shirer, *The Rise and Fall of the Third Reich*, p. 58.
15. Quoted in George J.W. Goodman, "The German Hyperinflation, 1923," Commanding Heights: The Battle for the World Economy, 2002. www.pbs.org.

16. Quoted in Richard Overy, ed., *The New York Times Complete World War II*. New York: Black Dog & Leventhal, 2013, p. 7.
17. Quoted in Goodman, "The German Hyperinflation, 1923."
18. Quoted in Richard Weikart, *Hitler's Ethic: The Nazi Pursuit of Evolutionary Progress*. New York: Palgrave MacMillan, 2009, p. 74.

Chapter Three: How Did Japanese Militarism Lead to the War in the Pacific?

19. Robert Higgs, "How US Economic Warfare Provoked Japan's Attack on Pearl Harbor," Independent Institute, May 1, 2006. www.independent.org.
20. Gordon W. Prange, *At Dawn We Slept: The Untold Story of Pearl Harbor*. New York: McGraw-Hill, 1981, p. 5.
21. Quoted in Prange, *At Dawn We Slept*, p. 5.
22. Quoted in Prange, *At Dawn We Slept*, p. 7.
23. Quoted in Prange, *At Dawn We Slept*, p. 364.
24. Quoted in Avalon Project, "Japanese Note to the United States, December 7, 1941," 2008. http://avalon.law.yale.edu.
25. Quoted in Avalon Project, "Japanese Note to the United States, December 7, 1941."

Chapter Four: How Did the Normandy Invasion Lead to Germany's Surrender?

26. Denys Schur, *The Second Front: Grand Strategy and Civil-Military Relations of Western Allies and the USSR, 1938–1945*. Monterey, CA: US Naval Postgraduate School, 2005. www.dtic.mil.
27. Quoted in Avalon Project, "The Tehran Conference, November 28–December 1, 1943," 2008. http://avalon.law.yale.edu.
28. Quoted in Kenneth Winchester, ed., *The Time-Life History of World War II*. New York: Barnes & Noble, 1995, p. 287.
29. S.L.A. Marshall, "First Wave at Omaha Beach," *Atlantic*, November 1960. www.theatlantic.com.
30. Quoted in Winchester, *The Time-Life History of World War II*, p. 295.
31. Quoted in Shirer, *The Rise and Fall of the Third Reich*, p. 1039.

32. Quoted in Shirer, *The Rise and Fall of the Third Reich*, p. 1040.
33. Quoted in Winchester, *The Time-Life History of World War II*, p. 374.

Chapter Five: How Did the Marshall Plan Revitalize Postwar Europe?

34. Quoted in Keith Lowe, *Savage Continent: Europe in the Aftermath of World War II*. New York: St. Martin's, 2012, pp. 7–8.
35. Quoted in Lowe, *Savage Continent*, pp. 9–10.
36. Quoted in George C. Marshall Foundation, "The Marshall Plan Speech." http://marshallfoundation.org.
37. Quoted in Nicolaus Mills, *Winning the Peace: The Marshall Plan and America's Coming of Age as a Superpower*. Hoboken, NJ: Wiley, 2008, p. 153.
38. Quoted in James Reston, "The Marshall Plan," *New York Times*, May 24, 1987. www.nytimes.com.
39. John Gimbel, *The Origins of the Marshall Plan*. Stanford, CA: Stanford University Press, p. 247.
40. Andrea Hiott, *Thinking Small: The Long, Strange Trip of the Volkswagen Beetle*. New York: Ballantine, 2012, p. 294.
41. Quoted in Peter J. Duignan and Lewis H. Gann, "The Marshall Plan," *Hoover Digest*, October 30, 1997. www.hoover.org.
42. Henry Kissinger, "Reflections on the Marshall Plan," *Harvard Gazette*, May 22, 2015. http://news.harvard.edu.

Books

David A. Andelman, *A Shattered Peace: Versailles 1919 and the Price We Pay*. Hoboken, NJ: Wiley, 2014.

Edward J. Drea, *Japan's Imperial Army: Its Rise and Fall*. Lawrence: University Press of Kansas, 2016.

Lawrence J. Haas, *Harry and Arthur: Truman, Vandenberg, and the Partnership That Created the Free World*. Lincoln, NE: Potomac, 2016.

Steve Twomey, *Countdown to Pearl Harbor: The Twelve Days to the Attack*. New York: Simon & Schuster, 2016.

Volker Ullrich, *Hitler: Ascent, 1889–1939*. New York: Knopf, 2016.

Internet Sources

George J.W. Goodman, "The German Hyperinflation, 1923," Commanding Heights: The Battle for the World Economy, 2002. www.pbs.org/wgbh/commandingheights/shared/minitextlo/ess_german hyperinflation.html.

Robert Higgs, "How US Economic Warfare Provoked Japan's Attack on Pearl Harbor," Independent Institute, May 1, 2006. www.independent.org/newsroom/article.asp?id=1930.

Henry Kissinger, "Reflections on the Marshall Plan," *Harvard Gazette*, May 22, 2015. http://news.harvard.edu/gazette/story/2015/05/reflections-on-the-marshall-plan.

S.L.A. Marshall, "First Wave at Omaha Beach," *Atlantic*, November 1960. www.theatlantic.com/magazine/archive/1960/11/first-wave-at-omaha-beach/303365.

Websites

D-Day, June 6, 1944 (www.army.mil/d-day). This website established by the US Army provides an overview of the 1944 invasion of France. Visitors to the site can read descriptions of the assaults on the five Normandy beaches, read biographies of the four American soldiers who earned the Congressional Medal of Honor for valor on D-day, and find numerous photographs of American soldiers carrying out the assault.

George C. Marshall Foundation (http://marshallfoundation.org). Maintained by the Lexington, Virginia, foundation that studies the work of Secretary of State George C. Marshall, the site contains numerous resources on the Marshall Plan and post–World War II Europe. The site includes the text of Marshall's 1947 speech at Harvard University announcing plans to rebuild Europe, as well as a video displaying images of battle-torn Europe.

International Churchill Society (www.winstonchurchill.org). Established to study the work of Winston Churchill, the society maintains an extensive website devoted to the accomplishments of the British prime minister. Visitors can find a biography of Churchill, covering his reaction to the Munich Agreement, his leadership during World War II, and his diplomatic achievements following the war. Visitors can download copies of *Finest Hour*, the society's publication that contains many scholarly articles on Churchill.

Interwar Period and Its Impacts on the World (www.mtholyoke.edu/~rapte22p/classweb/interwarperiod/index.html). Maintained by Mount Holyoke College in Massachusetts, this site provides an overview of the interwar period in Germany, focusing on the Treaty of Versailles, the failure of the Weimar government, the rise of the Nazis, and the appeasement of Hitler at Munich. Visitors can find descriptions of the events as well as photographs and political cartoons of the era.

Joseph Stalin: National Hero or Cold-Blooded Murderer? (www.bbc.co.uk/timelines/z8nbcdm). Maintained by the BBC, this website covers the life of Joseph Stalin, who ruled as Soviet dictator for more than thirty years. The site includes an extensive biography of Stalin, images of life in the Soviet Union during his rule, radio broadcasts by commentators discussing Stalin's life, political cartoons from the era, and video clips of historians discussing Stalin's impact on the twentieth century.

US Holocaust Museum (www.ushmm.org). The website of the museum in Washington, DC, includes many resources on the rise of the Nazi Party in Germany, including a biography of Adolf Hitler, a time line of events covering developments in Germany from 1933 to 1945, and a history of the Warsaw Ghetto Uprising, which led to the slaughter of Jews in Warsaw, as well as the eventual destruction of much of the Polish city by Nazi occupiers.

INDEX